The
Greater
Inheritance

an autobiography by **S**chrock **Mary**

First Printing 2009

Printed in the United States of America

1. Autobiography 2. Religion 3. Inspirational

ISBN 978-1-935298-24-3

Truth Book Publishers
824 Bills Rd
Franklin, IL 62638   TRUTH BOOK PUBLISHERS
www.truthbookpublishers.com

Cover design by Omar Schrock

Cover photo of Amish buggy and skies by James Wheeler
Photo of Amish lady by Tim Whitfield
Photo of Amish gentleman by Omar Schrock
All photos used by permission

All scripture is quoted from the King James Version

Acknowledgments

With deepest gratitude I express my sincere appreciation to my loving husband for his dedicated support, input, encouragement, and prayers for me while I was writing this book. Without him, so patiently going the extra mile, this task would have been extremely difficult, if not impossible.

A heartfelt thank you goes to our son Omar, who did an extraordinary job in designing the cover. May God bless him and his wife Tracy for their help and encouragement.

Also, to our daughters Rosa and husband Tom, and Loretta and husband Paul J., for their prayers, constructive criticism, support, and encouragement to continue when I was hesitant.

In addition, I thank our two youngest blessings, Nathan and Matthew, for their patience and help throughout this long process.

I shall not overlook our five adorable little grandsons so far, Timothy, Sean, Paul Jon, Kenny, and Johnathan, who are still too young to understand that books are written by real people!

Last, but not least, a very special thank you to my niece, Rhoda Bontrager, for her willingness, sacrifice, and much patience in editing and proofreading this book. Her expertise has been an enormous blessing, and greatly appreciated.

It is with great joy that I lovingly dedicate this book to my Lord and to each individual mentioned above.

Contents

Foreword

Have you ever been puzzled by the Amish people and their lifestyle? Ever wondered what it is like for those born and raised in the midst of a culture where dark clothes, black hats, horses, and buggies are a vital part of life? Their strangely secret lives and isolation from the rest of the world have always remained a mystery to you. Where old fashioned is a way of life and modern conveniences and the latest technologies are forbidden.

Have you wondered what they really believe about God? Why they practice excommunication and severe shunning? What the consequences are of breaking away from their peculiar religion?

Born into the Amish religion, my husband John and I have experienced the answers to all these perplexing questions, and more, first hand.

A few years ago, God burdened my heart to write a book, not only answering these questions, but primarily testifying of His life-changing work of grace in our lives. Eventually, I realized God would not allow me peace of mind unless I submitted to His call to tell others of His saving grace and how it has changed our lives forever. *Come and hear, all ye that fear God, and I will declare what he hath done for my soul* (Psalm 66:16).

Minor details have been added for clarification in chapters one, two, and three. The remaining chapters have very minimal added details. This is a true account, as I recall it, of our lives in the Old Order Amish religion and culture. Our experience is not necessarily representative of all Old Order Amish communities. However, each community shares a similar basic set of rules and regulations.

The names mentioned in italics have been changed. All others are identified by their real names.

While John and I are no longer a part of the Amish religion, we have no desire to belittle, slander, or seek revenge within these pages. Nor do we seek to draw sympathy, in any way, for the challenges God allowed us to experience for His glory.

We appreciate our rich heritage of a strong work ethic, honesty, and integrity.

However, the Amish religion and lifestyle is more than meets the eye. In this book, I endeavor to give you an honest inside perspective on a culture and religion often misinterpreted and misunderstood. The impression gained by the "outsider" is often contradicted by the true experience of the "insider."

Miraculously, God can work through our most difficult situations to make our lives complete in Him, when we place all the broken pieces at the Savior's feet.

The Author

The
Greater
Inheritance

an autobiography by **S**_**Mary**_ **chrock**

Chapter One

A Special Day

Another cold December night was yielding to the wee morning hours in our large Old Order Amish community in Buchanan County, Iowa in 1964. A fluffy blanket of snow covered the countryside under the twinkling sky, while the moon sent its last rays of light through the upstairs bedroom window of our two-story white farmhouse.

As a six-year-old girl, I was convinced *Dat's* (Dad's) five-thirty wake-up call echoed up the stairs much too early. I rolled over sleepily and snuggled under the soft comforter to enjoy a few last moments of coziness in the bed I shared with my eight-year-old sister, Alma. However, my pleasure was short lived when she reminded me it was the special school day we had been anticipating for several months.

Quickly, we hopped out of bed, our feet touching the cold wooden floor. I shivered as I slipped out of my warm nightgown into my navy Amish dress, buttoning it up swiftly. We made a dash for the stairway and quickly found ourselves beside the old wood-burning stove in the sparsely-furnished living room. There, we joined ten-year-old Jerry, the oldest of six children. We each pulled a straight-back chair up to the warm stove where the flames were flickering softly. I put on my knee-length, heavy black socks and black high-top shoes in preparation for the day.

Dat had already lit the gas lantern and marched out to the hog barn to begin the morning chores. *Mem* (Mom) hurriedly poked small pieces of firewood into the kitchen range to get it fired up before going out to help with the milking. The range needed to be hot enough to cook a quick breakfast later when she returned from the barn.

Meanwhile, Jerry and Alma wandered over to the corner of the kitchen to find their coats and boots. They chatted excitedly about the special day ahead as they struggled to close the hooks and eyes on their coats. Adding yellow chore gloves and black boots, Jerry topped off his outfit with his black wool hat, while Alma covered her head with a black wool headscarf. *Mem* soon had the lantern lit for Alma, and urged them both toward the door. Although they dreaded leaving the warmth of the kitchen, they opened the door and braved the cold outside. The fun of plodding through the snow soon caused them to forget the freezing temperature.

Dat was busy feeding the sows that had baby pigs. Many times as a little girl, I was quite impressed when I saw him carry two five-gallon buckets of feed to the mamma sows. I was confident that he was strong enough to do anything on the farm, no matter how difficult it was.

Soon his medium-build frame made long strides over to the big red barn where the muscular workhorses neighed softly as he entered the stable. They waited impatiently in anticipation of the oats and hay he would give them for breakfast. Nellie, our brown buggy horse, made sure old Prince, in the next stall, would not sneak one bite of her breakfast.

The Greater Inheritance

By then, Jerry had made the trek through the snow to the barn. He squinted as he entered when the bright beams of the gas lantern hanging in the stable struck his eyes. Instinctively, he made his way through the cow stable and over to the feeding alley. Grabbing a tin bucket, he began dipping ground feed from the big barrel in the corner. He poured a pile of grain at each stanchion (headlock) where the milk cows would soon be tied up. Once the door to the holding shed opened, the cows made a hasty entrance to their usual feeding spot. Most of them had a preferred stanchion and were trained to head straight to it when entering the stable. Jerry easily locked each cow in her place as they greedily gulped down their breakfast, oblivious to any surrounding activities.

Mem had now joined *Dat* and Jerry to help milk the herd of ten Holstein dairy cows by hand. When she was finished, she hurried back to the house to prepare a hot breakfast for everyone, while *Dat* and Jerry finished the last details in the barn.

Meanwhile, Alma, with a kerosene lantern in one hand and bucket in the other, had gone to the chicken house to feed and water the thirty-five laying hens. The water slopped from her bucket, freezing to her long skirt, as she carried it from the pump at the windmill to the chicken house. With several inches of snow to trudge through, it was a challenge for an eight-year-old to make the fifty to sixty-foot trek and still have much water left in the bucket. It was also an opportunity to have a little fun in the snow along the way.

Once inside the cozy chicken house, Alma enjoyed listening to the hens' cackling as they came running softly across the straw-bedded floor. They were eager to see what was for breakfast, and even bravely ate out of her hand when she offered it to them. Alma was thrilled with several that seemed to think they were her special pets and allowed her to hold them in her arms in unspoken communication. When all of them were contentedly scratching away at their grainy feast, she quietly slipped out the door. The eggs would be gathered after school, when the hens were finished laying eggs for the day.

While the outside chores were being done, I had the responsibility of looking after the three younger siblings in the house. I was barely older than my "captives" who were five-year-old Ervin, John who was three, and two-year-old Rachel. It was also my duty to have the table set for breakfast before *Mem* returned from the barn.

The sun was rising over the horizon as the chores were completed and everyone gathered around the table. *Mem's* short, stocky figure bustled about the kitchen as we helped her set the steaming breakfast on the table. After we bowed our heads for a customary silent prayer, we had a simple breakfast of eggs, fried potatoes, cooked oatmeal, milk, and bread and butter. Following breakfast, we knelt in prayer while *Dat* read the Morning Prayer from the German prayer book.

Mem quickly packed a lunch into three black tin lunch boxes for Jerry, Alma, and me. Meanwhile, *Dat* hurried to the barn to hitch Nellie to the black covered buggy. We were hoping she would not decide to be contrary and present one of her frequent balking spells. We had no time for stubbornness on that special morning.

On warmer days we walked the mile and a half to the one-room country schoolhouse. However, the frigid temperatures demanded a ride in the buggy for most of the students that day. Occasionally, we would catch a ride with neighbor *Will's* children when they took their buggy.

The Greater Inheritance

We arrived at the schoolhouse in due time without any trouble from Nellie. Our teacher, *Mrs. Nelson*, who was "English," as we called the non-Amish, had already fired up the round, wood-burning stove in the front of the classroom. Cold, stiff fingers made heavy wraps difficult to manage, but the compassionate *Mrs. Nelson* came to our rescue. She was kept busy helping to remove coats, gloves, wool scarves, black shawls, and bonnets or hats until all were comfortable.

The other students were as excited as we were about the day! With Christmas a few days away, the object of our eager anticipation was the special afternoon program.

After a few songs and morning classes were over, we ate our lunch, while noisily chatting about the program we would be performing shortly. Many of the parents were coming to enjoy the program as well, which added to our level of excitement.

As a kindergartener, I was a bit nervous, having to play the part of the Angel. Secretly though, I felt rather special wearing the big white, glittering angel wings my teacher had made for me. Years later she teased me about that day being the closest I ever got to being a real angel!

When *Mrs. Nelson* pulled back the curtain on the small makeshift stage, I stood as still as possible, for a kindergartener, and tried to be the "perfect angel." "Mary" and "Joseph" were sitting next to the manger, while other students were lined up on the stage reciting verses and poems. Everyone enjoyed singing the traditional Christmas carols and reenacting the event that took place so many years ago. The program went well, and *Mrs. Nelson* thanked each one for their participation.

At the tender age of six, I did not realize the significance of Christ's birth. I was much more drawn to the adorable little Amish-clad, homemade, faceless boy-doll lying in the manger. The tiny white shirt and black pants, complete with suspenders, were exceptionally adorable! I had very little knowledge of the Christ whom the doll represented, but one thing I knew: I deeply envied the privileged classmate who owned that precious doll. She had also brought a girl-doll dressed in a neat blue dress, black head covering, shawl, and bonnet. What's more, she was fortunate enough to possess a cute, miniature diaper bag her mother had made for her. It was the kind of doll and accessories that few were privileged to have, but would cause any little girl to covet. Oh, how I longed to have such a cute set to play with at home! However, my mother had enough sewing to do for her big family, without making dolls and doll clothes. Nevertheless, it was so incredibly cute that I never completely lost my desire to possess one, even as an adult!

After the program, the students exchanged gifts before dismissal time. Jerry, Alma, and I proudly presented the gift from our family to *Mrs. Nelson*. We watched eagerly as she unwrapped the quart jar of home-canned beef and a quart of *Mem's* canned peaches she had brought up from the basement that morning. She graciously thanked us for the unusual gift. We were happy to have something to give to her, be it ever so humble.

Our family finances were tight, and there were no extra funds for Christmas gifts for the family, let alone friends. Yet, occasionally on Christmas morning, *Dat* surprised us by placing a big juicy orange and a few pieces of hard candy on each plate at the breakfast table. What an exciting day it was! After all, not all children in the world had the privilege to enjoy an orange and candy for Christmas, we were told! We were blessed to have parents who gave what they could and taught us to appreciate whatever we received, no matter how great or small the gift.

Did You Know...

✓ At Christmas time, most Amish families celebrate the birth of Christ but to varying degrees, depending on the community in which they live. However, none of their churches allow the use of the traditional Christmas tree, which is perceived as a symbol of worldliness.

✓ Not all Amish schools had their own Amish teachers at the time I started school. Today, virtually all Amish schools have Amish teachers rather than "English" teachers. Amish teachers are generally recruited from the unmarried group between the ages of sixteen and twenty-one. Occasionally, a father or mother chooses to take the job, which brings in a very small side income. It was also an excellent job for single women in their late twenties or older who remained unmarried. Amish school buildings and curriculum expenses are supported by their own people through fundraisers and various other resources.

The Greater Inheritance

Chapter Two

Childhood

*I*n March, I had my seventh birthday, which came and went without incident. Birthdays were generally just another day, except for a playful "birthday spanking" from *Dat*. Occasionally, we were lucky enough to slip away just in time, delighting in having outwitted him! We enjoyed any extra attention to help make our day special, of course! We enjoyed being silly around *Dat* sometimes while he watched soberly, pretending to be unimpressed, until he had to burst out laughing and would say those "famous words" we were waiting for—*gricksht oft so shpells,* (do you often get such spells)?

Following the long winter months, spring, my favorite season, slowly began to appear. New life of plants, spring flowers, and budding trees could be seen everywhere, even baby chicks. We welcomed a special new life in April when sister Lizzie, child number seven, joined our family.

Spring also indicated it was soon gardening time. *Mem* became busier than ever. With canning, cooking, sewing, cleaning, laundry, and other endless jobs of a mother with seven children, she often turned to our teenage neighbor girls for help. The maid worked for very meager wages and even donated a considerable amount of her time.

Being neighborly and helping out in time of need is a common practice in most Amish communities.

Without modern conveniences, most tasks were very time consuming. However, we were used to it, and accepted it as the way of life. The lack of indoor plumbing and running water was not considered a hardship. Even going to the rustic outhouse was not too difficult. That was unless it was cold outside, or maybe after dark. In my little imaginative mind, I just knew there were "grisly monsters" hiding behind the nearby trees after dark. Alma was usually compassionate, grabbing a flashlight to join me on the terrifying 60-feet trek down the wooden plank path leading to our destination!

We were each given our own responsibilities at a young age. Some of my duties included washing the dishes, watching baby Lizzie for *Mem*, and pulling weeds from the many rows of vegetables in the garden during the summer months.

We rarely had to mow our yard since we had it fenced in, making it convenient to let the young calves graze on the lush green grass. Sometimes they even ate things not intended for them, such as the time when *Mem* was washing Alma's hair. She had Alma lying on the open concrete porch with her long, dark hair draped over the edge into a big basin of water on the steps. One of the calves was curious about all the activity taking place and ambled over to sniff things out. *Mem,* busy with the task at hand, ignored the nosy black and white bovine at first. Then, without warning, the creature swished out her big gray tongue, snatched up, and swallowed Alma's white head covering, which *Mem* had placed on the porch. *Mem* shrieked, *"Shoft dich doe raus"* (get out of here)! But she was seconds too late. It was gone, never to be retrieved! What a shock! I was horrified! It was her only head covering, besides her good one for school and her very best black one for church. *Mem* went searching for an old tattered covering for her to wear until she had time to make a new one. She would not think of letting her daughter run without one, not even for a day. The head covering, or prayer cap, was mandatory in the Amish religion according to their understanding of I Corinthians 11.

Whenever my siblings and I found a spare moment, and the weather was not too sultry, we enjoyed playing in the hayloft. What fun it was to make tunnels through the huge piles of hay, or between the bales, for an exciting game of hide and seek!

My sisters and I occasionally had great fun playing dolls with the little kittens in the barn. A burlap bag made a wonderful "blanket" in which to neatly wrap our "babies." We would cradle them in our arms and sing them to sleep, only to have them dash away in a flash if something frightened them. We would have to either fetch them again or decide the game was over until some other day.

We learned how to entertain ourselves with various yard games as well. Red rover, andy over, baseball, and tag were just a few of the games we enjoyed. During the winter months, we enjoyed a lot of sledding after school and an occasional game of fox and geese in the snow, if our chores were finished in time.

Outdoor toys with wheels were rare, except for the little red wagon. It served many purposes, from being used as a child's racing vehicle to hauling a basketful of laundry to the clothesline for *Mem*. It was also the perfect "hay wagon" when the boys wanted to play "horses." With Ervin holding on to one side of the little wagon tongue, and John on the other, Jerry had an energetic team of "horses" with which to put up his "hay." The only harnesses he needed were several long strands of baling twine for the reins. By pulling tall grass, they could quickly fill their wagon with "hay" and haul it off to a make-believe barn somewhere. The greatest excitement took place when the team would occasionally become "spooked" about something and "run away," upsetting the wagon and scattering the hay! At times, my sisters and I could not resist getting involved in the fun too.

There was never reason for boredom, even during the winter months, since we were trained to be creative and invent our own fun and games. I am thankful that good character and an innovative mind were important traits in my parents' view of child training.

Family mealtime was a time when character training was implemented. Our family was trained to eat whatever was set before us, even though it was usually very limited in variety. There were very few things on the table that did not come from our garden, fresh or canned. The menu was not "Take it, or leave it," but simply "Take it!" Under *Mem's* watchful eye, we quickly learned that skipping a helping from a less favorable dish would only mean more leftovers in the next meal. I can still hear her state the rules concerning leftovers, in our Pennsylvania Dutch dialect, *"Von mir all bisel nema, dann is es glei all"* (If we all take a little, it will soon be all gone). *Dat* always took a generous helping of leftovers, to be a good example to his crew around the table.

Very little food was ever discarded. *Mem* considered the wasting of food a serious mismanagement of God's provision for us. She tried to pass these convictions on to her children. If we wasted anything, she was quick to remind us that God might someday let us suffer starvation as a punishment. We were not allowed to be fussy eaters, and the words "I don't like it" were not to be uttered at our family table. I came to appreciate that training, though many years later, when rearing my own family.

Did You Know...

✓ Although many Amish churches allow their people to have bicycles, many do not. Our community considered them much too modern.

✓ In general, Amish adults and children alike are very hard-working and honest people. Children learn to work as young as two years old. Honesty is an important character trait ingrained in Amish children.

The Greater Inheritance

Chapter Three

New Home

*I*n the spring of 1966, our family experienced a life-changing event. My parents decided to take a rare weekend trip to Bowling Green, Missouri, traveling by bus. Only baby Lizzie had the privilege of going along that time. Our neighbor girl, *Susie,* came to stay with the rest of us in their absence. *Susie's* brother came only to help with morning and evening chores in the barn.

The change in our routine was interesting to us, and life continued without any major incidents. That was until the day my parents planned to arrive home, after having been gone for four days. That morning there was great excitement in the air. The chores and breakfast were done in record time. Even washing the dishes was accomplished with unusual enthusiasm and without arguments about whose turn it was.

Time seemed to stand still as we watched the road for the first sign of an approaching vehicle. At last, someone shrieked, *"Doe kumma sie"* (Here they come)! We all dashed out the door and down the sidewalk leading to the little yard gate. There we paused to wait for *Dat* and *Mem* to unload their luggage and dismiss the hired driver.

We were too bashful to talk or express excitement around "English" people, so we kept our distance until he was out of sight. We did not want to risk having to speak English, as we were much more comfortable with the customary Pennsylvania Dutch dialect.

When all of us were back in the house, it was difficult to know who to listen to as each of us eagerly competed for our parents' attention. We were also happy to see baby Lizzie again. How we had missed her baby chatter and giggles while she was away!

Eventually, *Mem* got a brief update of the week from *Susie*, and then released her from babysitting duties. When the atmosphere settled down, it was *Dat* and *Mem's* turn to give a report on the trip to Missouri. That was when we became aware that it had been, in reality, more than a casual trip to visit relatives. They proceeded to announce that we were moving to Missouri in the near future. For various reasons, they had decided that rearing their family in that particular Amish community was a wise choice.

Being too young to understand all that such a move would entail, it sounded rather exciting to me. On second thought, it became more alarming, even a bit scary, to think about attending a new school and making new friends! What would it be like? Would the other children be kind to newcomers? It was of great comfort to know that we would have an Amish teacher, with whom we were somewhat acquainted. She had also moved to Missouri from Iowa that year.

Moving day came at nearly the end of the summer. By some means, *Dat* generated the money to hire two truckers with semi-trailers to move all our household furniture, as well as all our livestock, to Missouri. That day was a bit unsettling to my siblings and myself when our home seemingly turned into a busy "bee hive." Neighbors and friends gathered to help carry furniture out of the house and load it, along with numerous pieces of farm machinery, onto one of the semi-trailers. The cows and horses were loaded onto the second truck.

Maggie, our family collie, was tucked in there somewhere as well. Oh, how we hoped she would arrive safely at our new home. We could not imagine life without her!

By the time everything was loaded, the day was nearly spent. It was time to bid our farewells to the only family and friends we children had ever known in our Iowa home. In our excitement, saying good-bye was not as difficult for us as it was for my parents, I am sure. I did not understand when I saw *Grosmommy* (Grandma) wipe away her tears. We were the ones leaving friends, cousins, and our familiar surroundings. *So why is she crying?* I wondered. I did not realize we would miss each other once we lived in Missouri and they were still back in Iowa.

Dat rode to our new home with one of the drivers in the big trucks, while *Grosdawdy* (Grandpa) rode in the other. The rest of us, along with *Grosmommy,* rode on the train, which was a new experience for my siblings and me. Of course, we were too excited to sleep, even on the comfortable reclining seats.

The special treats *Mem* brought along to ease the uncomfortable feeling of leaving friends and familiar surroundings added to our excitement. Nevertheless, we were not allowed to have any treats until we had some sleep. One special treat was a box of Cheerios. We very rarely had the privilege of enjoying such luxuries!

By and by, we managed to get some sleep, and morning came bright and early. It was Cheerio time! How we enjoyed them! *Mem* had also packed a few other finger snacks to munch on along the way.

The train sped rapidly down the tracks as we watched the countryside fly swiftly by. We knew our trip was almost over when the train slowed to a crawl as it rolled into the depot. We eagerly gathered our luggage and prepared to exit the coach. We soon found the "English" driver; he was appointed to take us several miles out into the country, around the curves and down a dusty road to our new home. We watched anxiously for the first glimpse of the farm.

Then, suddenly, up ahead we spotted a small house and an old weathered barn. "There it is, children!" *Mem* announced joyfully. The house looked so much smaller then we had expected, and the barn did not appear very impressive either. But *Mem* assured us we would be fine, even though living quarters were sure to be extremely cramped. "Maybe someday we will be able to build a new house," she encouraged us.

Coming to a halt in the driveway we quickly dismissed our mixed feelings, and dashed off in different directions. Naturally, our chief goal was to find Maggie, to confirm that she had indeed arrived safely. To our joy, we found her in good condition, although crouched underneath the porch and nervous about all the commotion and new surroundings.

We eagerly explored the house and found there were only two bedrooms, a very small kitchen and pantry, a small living room, and a tiny mudroom. There was also an unfinished attic that would serve as a room if needed, and a very small basement.

In spite of our family increasing in size during the subsequent years, we were forced to endure those cramped living conditions longer than expected. God allowed us to experience many valuable lessons in patience, endurance,

The Greater Inheritance

sharing, and thriftiness—lessons often not learned in a life of ease and prosperity.

Dat managed to find a place in the small and unimpressive barn to feed the horses and milk the cows. The milking had to be done in shifts, since there was room for only a few at a time. The little creek behind the barn conveniently furnished the water supply for all the livestock.

Since we had no indoor plumbing, we depended on the cistern beside the back porch for our water supply to the house. We merely had to step out onto the open porch, pump water into a bucket, and carry it into the house. Hot water was obtained by heating teakettles or big pots of water on top of the kitchen woodstove or on the kerosene stove.

We did our laundry in the little washhouse, a few feet from the back porch. The water was carried from the pump to the big, black cast iron kettle outside the washhouse. It did not take long to build a fire under it to heat the water, which was then carried to the wringer washer in the washhouse. This preparation for washing clothes usually took an hour or more. Generally, doing laundry from start to finish could consume most of a day, and was normally done once a week.

All the clothes were then hung on the long clothesline underneath the huge maple trees surrounding the house. In cold weather the clothes were often left outside longer while they freeze-dried, then brought inside to finish drying.

School started a few weeks after we moved. We usually walked the mile and a quarter to school, unless our good old neighbor, *Bill,* came along in his red 1950s-model truck. We soon learned we could always depend on him to offer us a ride. He did not seem to mind cramming the seat full beside him, while a couple of us rode in the back of the truck. We appreciated him, as well as other "English" neighbors, who frequently showed such kindness and shortened our boring walks to and from school. Those rides were especially helpful on mornings when we were running slightly behind schedule. When we had a late start, *Mem* commanded us to not only walk very fast, but also run much of the way, if we were not fortunate enough to catch a ride. Promptness was a major issue in our family, and a "tardy" marked on our report card was entirely unacceptable to my parents. As a result, in all eight years of schooling, my siblings and I always acquired a perfect A in that category.

Did You Know...

✓ Seldom, if ever, do Amish children hear the words "I love you" from their parents. Expressing affection past the baby stage is rare, although I have known a few families who experienced that blessing. It is not a normal part of their cultural practices. Kindness, along with food, shelter, clothing, and medical attention provided to the children, is considered evidence of love in many families.

Chapter Four

Hard Times

*B*y 1968 we had enjoyed our new school for a while, and formed some pleasant memories of those years. Nevertheless, because we were an unregenerate group of boys and girls, not having the true love of God in our hearts, we also made some not-so-pleasant memories. Even so, I believe God used some of those circumstances to prepare me for His future plan for my life.

Because of our meager food supply we had very simple school lunches, such as a molasses or apple butter sandwich, milk, an apple, and a piece of cake without icing. On rare occasions, we had canned peaches or mackerel (fish) sandwiches. On those days, we found it hard to wait for lunchtime. We were having something special! Once or twice a year we had a sandwich of the peanut butter left over from the church lunch when church services were held at our house. White crackers, graham crackers, brown sugar, chocolate chips, nuts, and any kind of cheese were just a few of the ordinary cooking "necessities" that were virtually nonexistent at our house. They were just too expensive on our insufficient income. Baking our own bread helped considerably with the food budget, because our family could easily consume five or six loaves a week.

It was difficult to understand how our classmates could have such lavish lunches. I assumed their families were simply abnormally rich. They usually had a cheese and bologna sandwich, a hamburger, or even a piece of pie. *Why can we not have that? Why is God not blessing our family in the way He blesses others, since we are Amish too?* I wondered repeatedly.

Our clothes also left much to be desired. My brothers' boots were plastered with so many patches where holes had developed that eventually it was a little difficult to recognize the original boots. Understandably, there was no money for new boots. We each had only two or three sets of school clothes, which we alternated weekly. We knew we were perceived by others as a less than prosperous family, and were easily intimidated by those who desired to dominate the Amish society.

Our backward social status soon earned our family ruthless mockery from our schoolmates, who had never experienced severe poverty and intimidation. Consequently, we began dreading each new school day. Although *Dat* and *Mem* were saddened by the treatment we endured at school, no amount of crying or begging to stay home ever proved successful. There was comfort in knowing that, as siblings, we could depend on the support of each other. However, we were rather glad if we woke up with a tummy ache, a bad cold, or any justifiable reason to skip a day of school.

At the time, I did not realize that God saw each tear and cared each time our hearts were broken because of ridicule and rejection from classmates who often refused to play with us at school or after church on Sundays.

Though finances were very tight, men working away from the farm, other than in construction work or sawmills, was not a favorable option in the eyes of the church leaders. Back then, the farm income was expected to suffice, in spite of some families having twelve to fifteen children. Today, many Amish families are supported by an additional income from a home business or employment apart from farming.

Sadly, our family's financial situation worsened before it eventually improved. When I was almost ten years old, Sadie joined our family, being born at home with the aid of a midwife. Baby Sadie was the joy of our family, a happy and healthy little girl. However, one day when she was a year old, she began running a temperature. It was steadily rising by the next day, and all efforts to reduce the fever failed. Humanly speaking, my parents did not need another financial burden. However, when the high temperature caused baby Sadie to go into convulsions, terrifying all of us, they realized the urgency of seeking medical help immediately. At the hospital, she was diagnosed with staph infection or viral pneumonia, an infection causing her to become gravely ill. More than once, the doctors did not give us much hope that she would survive the stubborn infection, which did not appear to respond well to medication.

Most of the time, my parents stayed with her at the hospital, which was about sixteen miles away, while a neighbor girl stayed with us children at home. I remember *Mem* coming home briefly one time to see the rest of the family and freshen up, then go back to the hospital again. *Dat* came home a few times to check up on several necessary duties. One night he was awakened with a message to come back to the hospital immediately, as baby Sadie had taken a turn for the worse. According to the doctors' outlook, we all feared we were going to lose her that night. With heavy hearts, we waited for a report the next morning. As children, we did not realize we could take our burdens to the Lord in prayer. But again, God miraculously spared our baby sister one more night.

Baby Sadie was kept heavily sedated until she started recovering. We rejoiced when we heard that her condition was finally improving, though ever so slowly. But my parent's trial was not over yet. Since baby Sadie's little body had become dependent on the sedative drugs, she had a very difficult time adjusting when the doctors tried to decrease the dosage. The poor little soul cried almost nonstop for a couple of days and nights as *Mem, Dat,* and the nurses took turns holding and rocking her, in an effort to comfort her somehow. What a dreadfully helpless feeling they must have experienced. After having been in the hospital for three weeks, she recovered enough to enable my parents to bring her home. Such a glad reunion it was!

Today, as a mother herself, Sadie still suffers from respiratory problems because of that illness. Nevertheless, it has not made the slightest dent in her remarkably sweet and loving spirit. I am deeply grateful that God spared our precious sister. Surely, He must have a special plan for her life.

Did You Know...

✓ Not all Amish households are as financially challenged as my family was growing up. Some have much more generous incomes, especially those living in areas with fewer restrictions by the church, or in tourist areas.

✓ Because family planning is prohibited, many Amish families consist of twelve to fifteen children. Consequently, the women generally cannot afford to give birth in a hospital. A well-trained midwife is called into the home for assistance. Normally, only the births with anticipated complications take place at a hospital.

✓ Many less-conservative Amish communities have very respectful children and young people. There, families generally do not experience the mockery that some endure in the more conservative communities. Most of the very conservative communities are quite intolerant of personal and financial differences among their people, commonly manifested in rather problematic attitudes.

The Greater Inheritance

Chapter Five

Growing Up

A little over a year later, we welcomed baby Lovina into the family, also born at home. She had tiny features and was especially cute! Truthfully, as a mother even now, she still possesses that blessing.

We worked hard every summer when we were on school break, with occasional fun times too. After a week of hard work, we always looked forward to our in-between Sunday, since we had church only every two weeks. As we grew older, that was one of the few times we had the energy or time to play. On those Sundays we enjoyed hearing *Dat* read from the German Bible for hours in a singsong style. The little ones, whose attention span had quickly expired, usually stood on a chair pulled up beside *Dat*'s rocker and found great pleasure in repeatedly running a big comb through his head of graying hair. However, they learned it did not work so well on his long beard. We equally enjoyed hearing *Dat* sing Dutch children's songs at Sunday naptime when he would rock the youngest ones to sleep.

There was usually only one vacation day from farm work for each of the children in the summer, a day we all looked forward to with great enthusiasm. That was normally the only time of the year that we were allowed to go to town. In most Amish parents' opinion, children did not have much business in such a worldly place.

We preferred to have our annual trip to town on a day that the local hardware store had "Peanut Days." They had all-you-can-eat free peanuts in the shells for their customers to enjoy. I remember four or five of us children piling into the buggy with *Dat,* and off to town we would go. We could hardly wait to get our hands into those wheelbarrows full of delicious peanuts! It was a very rare treat for us, indeed! A stop at Dairy Queen for a 25¢ ice cream cone was the climax of the exciting adventure. We were fascinated by all the "fancy English" things in the stores. It was extremely different from life on the farm. What a delightful day it was!

We were even foolish enough at times to wish that we would have to see the doctor for some reason, which would necessitate a trip to town. There were no visits to the dentist either. We were all blessed with healthy teeth in general but if one of us had a minor toothache, the remedy was usually, "Drink more milk." *Mem* insisted that the abundance of milk we drank prevented many tooth decays.

To keep us busy, there was the huge garden with plenty of weeds to pull. We picked and canned bushels and bushels of green beans, peas, and corn each summer. Then there were many long rows of strawberries to pick too. *Mem* sold most of those and some beans and corn for a little additional income. Eggs were another source of a few dollars, occasionally.

Each summer went by quickly, and September brought another burst of excitement. We would be heading back to school again. Eventually, circumstances at school improved considerably in my seventh and eighth grade years. Our family was actually able to enjoy school again.

We credited some of that improvement to John, the teacher at that time. He was also the deacon of our church. He apparently had eyes in the back of his head, and supervised well at all times, especially during recess. We appreciated that more than he will ever know. He had a strong hand of discipline, yet he was always kind and caring. Unfortunately, he was able to teach only a year or two, as I recall. I had a couple of good teachers during my school years, but I would dare say John was my favorite one.

At age fourteen I graduated from eighth grade, along with my classmates, David, Daniel, and my ever-loyal friend Katie. There was no schooling for an Amish student beyond eighth grade. Hurray! I was out of school at last! I had reached that long-desired goal. No more school for me! I was very happy, indeed, although my last year was probably one of my most enjoyable years in school. There was no intimidation from older students, and the unity among the student body had improved dramatically by then.

The first fall I was out of school, little Anna joined us, making our family of ten children complete. She was also born at home, and I remember the doctor making a house call to check on *Mem* and the baby. Anna was special to me, since I was out of school and able to help care for her every day.

I turned fifteen the next spring and had the wonderful privilege of going to Indiana with *Dat* for a cousin's wedding. I made some friends while there and enjoyed spending some time with the cousins, whom we did not see very often.

We stayed at Aunt Mary's house the night of the wedding, and we had store-bought cereal for breakfast the next morning. I specifically remember that, because I did not take any cereal for this simple reason: I did not know how to go about opening that stubborn bag inside a new box of cereal. Rather than risking embarrassment, I said I did not care for any, and passed it on to the one next to me. We never had store-bought cereal at home. That was only for rich people. Our cereal was either cooked oatmeal or wheat, or homemade grapenuts and such. I still think of that incident at times when I open a new box of cereal in our own home now!

We were gone only a few days that time, but it seemed a long time to be away from the family. I really missed them and got quite homesick. It was probably my first out-of-state trip since I had been five years old.

I spent the next few years at home, continuing to develop my culinary skills and learning all the traditional skills necessary to become a good housewife and mother someday.

The traditional art of quilting was a skill that *Mem* neither took pleasure in, nor considered necessary to teach us. In her opinion, there was always more important work to do. As a result, we never learned to enjoy a quilting bee as some did. Despite that, I have a love for beautiful quilts!

I was also frequently asked to be a *maud:* to help a mother who was overwhelmed with a big family and a massive load of housework besides her sewing and gardening. Sometimes it meant helping a mother who had a new baby and several toddlers to care for. A *maud* would do laundry, help cook, clean the house, work in the garden, or anything with which the housewife could not keep up. I did not mind that job if I was not required to stay so long that I got homesick. A two-week job was not unusual.

Eight years after moving to Missouri, prospects of a new house began to develop. The material used to frame the house was salvaged mostly from a huge building our family dismantled in a neighboring town. That was a great deal of work, but it significantly cut the building costs, which appeared to be the only possible way of building a new house.

Every member of our family helped pull thousands of nails to prepare the lumber for use. Although we all had a hand in bringing the new house to reality, *Dat* hired a carpenter crew to build it. They happened to be Bishop Eicher and his five sons. We cooked dinner for them every day when they were working on the house. We also had a few workdays similar to the Amish barn raisings, which we called "frolics." That was when the neighbors and relatives or anyone in the community could volunteer to help with the building. It was always exciting to survey the major progress made by the end of the day. After a few months the house was enclosed, and the windows and outside doors were in place.

When the carpenters' job was done, we painted the walls and finished the hardwood oak floors. Obviously, there was no electricity, phone lines, or plumbing to install. The wood trim for the windows and doors had to wait until later. We were eager to move in as soon as possible.

For many years, we had not known if the new house would ever become a reality. Consequently, it was a very joyful occasion when we moved into the huge, white two-story house with six bedrooms. It was built right next to the old house, which was eventually demolished.

Our furniture seemed to almost disappear in the spacious new kitchen and living room. The big summer kitchen was also a plus. That kitchen, with its big windows, was cooler and breezier than the main kitchen during the hot summer. We moved the kitchen supplies and utensils to the summer kitchen in late spring since it was cooler out there. That was where we cooked dinner for the men on the neighborhood harvesting crew when it was our turn. We could then close up the main kitchen until fall, at which time we moved back in there where it was easier to keep warm. It was especially convenient to have the six-by-nine-foot pantry between the two kitchens, in which to store the food, pots, and pans.

On the first floor, was my parents' bedroom and a bedroom for Lovina and Anna. The rest of us could sleep in three of the four bedrooms upstairs. One room was reserved for storage of family keepsakes and accumulations.

Did You Know...

✓ Very few Amish families live in one area all their life. Most families move numerous times from state to state or from one community to another for various reasons. Normally, it is because of disunity among the members or being disgruntled with the *Ordnung* (church rules). Rarely is it for economic reasons.

✓ The Amish philosophy is that a formal school education is worldly and unnecessary. It is believed that a boy, who is expected to become a devoted husband and farmer for life, ought to work side by side with his *dat* until he is prepared to enter into marriage. Likewise, a girl should work closely with her *Mem* until she too becomes a housewife and *mem*. For young people to further their education in school would be considered a waste of time and deprive them of valuable hands-on learning of life skills.

✓ The Amish pay school and other taxes like everyone else, except they apply for and receive an exemption from social security taxes.

✓ Old Order Amish (conservative Amish) people originally did not have cars, electricity, and phones in their houses. Using the English neighbor's phone was a very common occurrence. However, today many have their own cell phones, or a community phone in an outbuilding. Most will now freely ride in cars anywhere for any reason, but will not drive.

Our new six-bedroom house

View of our new house from the barn

The Greater Inheritance

Chapter Six

Seventeen

*T*he next spring, March 1975, I turned seventeen, which meant I was approaching some major events in my life. I was now old enough to join the youth group. Every Sunday evening the young people would gather to sing and socialize at a home where church services had been held that day. At seventeen, one was also considered to be of dating age.

Then in April, I joined the instruction class for baptism. I remember the Sunday when I joined the class that church services were at the Borntrager's house. When Bishop Eicher announced the beginning of the service, a hush fell over the congregation. Immediately, a hymn from the German *Ausbund* (hymnal) was announced. One of the men in the living room, where all the married men and young boys were seated, lifted his voice to begin the first stanza. He was the lead singer for the rest of the hymn by singing out the first syllable of each line, after which the congregation joined him.

As that was taking place, all the ministers in attendance filed out to a counseling room prepared for them in another part of the house. That was also when four seventeen-year-old young men, Ernest, Joe, David, and Daniel got up to follow them to the counseling room. Since

I was seventeen also, I was expected to follow them as well. The ministers spent the next thirty to forty minutes teaching us the first two of eighteen Articles of Faith from the Dordrecht Confession.

The Articles were written in the city of Dordrecht in Holland in 1632, and are used by most Amish churches today to instruct baptismal candidates. Those first two articles consisted of teachings about creation and the fall of man. The next eight classes covered the remaining sixteen articles concerning many subjects. Some of those subjects were the crucifixion, repentance, baptism, the church of God, ordination of ministers, the Lord's Supper, foot washing, holy matrimony, nonresistance, excommunication, shunning, and the resurrection of the dead. For five months, we attended those classes every two weeks during church services. I was very nervous at first, since I was the only girl and the four boys were all cousins to each other. Having another girl join us would have been much more pleasant for me, but there were none of the same age in our district.

Being extremely shy, I found it very intimidating to speak to any boys, except my brothers or cousins. Besides, I was taught that any decent girl would not pay public attention to boys not related to her. As a result, I hardly ever communicated with the boys in our instruction class. It was just far too intimidating.

Again, I worked hard all summer, helping with the farming and gardening, picking and canning produce. My sisters and I picked bushels and bushels of peas until we thought our backs were in danger of being permanently stooped over. At times, we could almost convince ourselves that those rows of peas were at least a quarter of a mile long! Of course *Mem* did not agree.

We found sweet relief as we sat under the shade trees enjoying a time of pleasant fellowship as sisters, working together for many hours while mindlessly popping the peas out of the pods. Usually, it was an all-day process to get all the peas into quart canning jars. *Mem* was happy if we ended up with fifty to sixty quarts of peas on the basement shelves.

Our family was always kept very busy, which I am sure was to our own benefit. Meanwhile, our minds were usually busy as well. My baptism day coming up at the end of August seemed to occupy my mind daily. Then, my thoughts were suddenly diverted one Sunday evening in July, about a month before I was to be baptized.

The youth group had gathered for a hymn singing at the home where church services had been held that day. After the singing, my heart nearly jumped into my throat and butterflies filled my stomach when two young men approached me with a message. In the customary manner, they called me aside from the small group of girls I was with outside the house, and privately informed me that John Schrock wished to give me a ride to my home that evening. "Is that all right with you?" they asked. They did not have to wait long for my answer. "Yes, that would be all right," I assured them. Although I had never met John personally, his sisters were good friends of mine, and I knew their family of fifteen children had an honorable reputation in the community. I was honored and delighted that he would consider me for a date even though our lifestyles were of great contrast in some aspects, particularly in the financial realm.

Having the opportunity to be the messenger between prospective couples always appeared to be a delight to any of the young men. The messengers gleefully took my reply back to John, where he was nervously waiting outside the barn for my response. I am sure he was relieved to receive a positive reply, since it was a first time experience for him in the realm of dating. Not knowing me very well, he was not sure what to expect. However, he desired to become better acquainted with me and was encouraged by his sisters, as well as several of his peers, to do so.

Since both of us were very shy, we had only brief conversations on our forty-five-minute ride home in his buggy. My first few words to him were a comment about the beautiful, moonlit evening. He agreed with a friendly smile. *This is so romantic!* I mused to myself. I tried to hide my giddy emotions. I could hardly believe he had asked me for a date. Even though I had dated others previously, that date was more significant to me than any others had been! In my immature, youthful mind, I suspected I would be the envy of several of my friends, and gleefully found a sense of pleasure in that.

When we arrived at my home, we entered the house quietly, not wanting to disturb my parents and the younger siblings, who were already in bed. I carefully lit the kerosene lamp sitting on the dresser in the living room, and turned it down low. We then had the dimly lit room to ourselves for the evening, as was the custom in our community. We had never spoken a word to each other prior to that evening, so we were strangers, indeed. However, we enjoyed each other's company, while rummaging through every nook and cranny of our intellects in search of a sensible conversation starter. Since we both were only seventeen, we did not start dating more frequently until several months later.

The typical dating style in our community was an occasional date, or every two weeks at the beginning. That would soon become a weekly event if the couple decided to

The Greater Inheritance

continue their relationship. Sunday evenings and special occasions, such as weddings, were the only times any dates were permitted by the church in our community.

Did You Know...

- ✓ *Rumspringa,* or "sowing wild oats," is not freely accepted in the majority of Amish churches. Nevertheless, it is rampant in some areas, including in some of the most conservative churches. All humans have the sin nature, despite any *Ordnung* (church rules). Evidently, forced compliance will not change the heart.

- ✓ Normally, an Amish youth will leisurely "date around," until he eventually marries. Surprisingly, some of the more liberal Amish churches have the most conservative courtship standards. Their standards, of course, are ridiculed by some conservative churches, which have surprisingly low courtship standards. Go figure! A few communities even allow bed courtship.

Living room where John and I had our first date—only no furniture in it now

Front porch steps—a favorite dating spot for us

Chapter Seven

Church Membership

*S*unday morning, August 24, 1975 dawned at last, promising a hot and humid day. When *Dat* called, *"Boova, mait, zeit fa uf shtay!"* (Boys, girls, time to get up!), I jumped out of bed, dressed quickly, and hurried downstairs. All summer I had been eagerly waiting for this special day! I soberly pondered the event that would bring me to a major milestone of my life. I desperately tried to grasp the reality of it all.

However, I could not waste any time daydreaming. I knew I did not want to be late in joining *Dat,* Jerry, Ervin, and John in the barn for the morning milking. Grabbing our milking aprons from the hooks in the mudroom, Alma, Rachel, and I hurried off to the barn.

Dat finished feeding and tying up the last cow in her stall. Grabbing a one-legged stool and a bucket, I marched over to Alice, one of the three cows I milked every morning and evening. She was obviously unimpressed with my urgent demands to hurriedly get situated for the hobbles. I still had Judy and Beauty to milk, and had no time for sluggish bovine behavior. All of our milk cows were known by name, and at times, a few of our beef cattle even earned a name, depending on their nature or disposition.

Milking time was usually when we enjoyed catching up with each other on the latest community news. But, since it was Sunday morning, everyone was concentrating on being done as soon as possible. My bucket filled with streams of warm, foamy milk, while my thoughts turned again to the day ahead.

I aspired to have my heart prepared for baptism and the changes it would bring into my life. Tradition had taught me that the step I was preparing to take was expected of me. I was eager, yet quite apprehensive about making the transition into church membership. I certainly wanted to please my parents, the church, and God as much as possible, thus the need to be baptized and join the church. My assumption was that God would certainly be pleased with me when the day was over. If only I could be confident that He indeed loved me unconditionally … "Ouch!" A vigorous swish of Alice's tail in my face jerked me back to reality. She evidently did not appreciate the pesky barn flies any more than I did.

My knowledge of the Bible was very limited. While I was privileged to have my own German New Testament, and read a chapter from it every Sunday at home, I comprehended very little of the truth in German. Since we spoke only a dialect of German, the German Bible was typically more difficult to understand than the English for most Amish people.

I did know that God is holy and almighty, and I was very afraid of disobeying Him. He seemed so far away at times. I often imagined Him sitting up there in heaven, watching my every move, letting me live in peace when I was obedient, but ready to strike me down when I failed or displeased Him in any matter. I was never sure that He would hear my prayers. Yet, God surely must have cared enough to allow me to be born into an Amish family, I thought. For that, I was to consider myself a very fortunate girl, I heard the preachers say frequently. How I longed to know God better and to have His stamp of approval on my life, if possible. I supposed being baptized would surely be a big step in that direction.

I had so much to think about while I milked one cow after another. We were soon finished, and everyone hurried back to the house where *Mem* had prepared a simple breakfast of farm fresh eggs and cooked wheat cereal.

By then Lizzie, Sadie, Lovina, and Anna were up also, and everybody found their usual place around the table. After bowing our heads for a silent prayer, *Dat's* soft shuffle in his chair and the clearing of his throat signaled the end of prayer time. Breakfast was finished quickly, since no one wanted to suffer the embarrassment of getting to church late.

As on most Sunday mornings, the dishes were quickly cleared away, and everyone hurried to get dressed in their Sunday best. I ran upstairs, excited about wearing my new, handmade, black dress with a sheer white starched cape and apron over it, which was the traditional dress code for baptism. I neatly twisted and pinned my hair up in a bun, and placed my new black head covering over it. After tying it under my chin, I checked to make sure the tails of the bow were not longer than allowed. I did not want to suffer the embarrassment of *Mem* correcting it (again) in front of my peers at church. As the typical Amish girl, I primped and double-checked in the mirror to make sure everything fit as neatly as possible without violating the church *Ordnung*.

Properly dressed for the day's event, Alma and I hurried downstairs to help Sadie, Lovina, and Anna get dressed for the day. Rachel and Lizzie were old enough to care for themselves. After *Mem* was dressed and had taken care of various motherly details, she checked each little face for any telltale signs of breakfast. She smoothed back any stray hair peeking out from under their black head coverings placed over their neatly braided hair. The warm summer days meant no shoes were needed for the younger ones. Excited and barefooted, they grabbed their black bonnets, which were mandatory when going on the road, and pitter-pattered across the wooden kitchen floor to the front porch. How cute and innocent they were in their little black Sunday dresses and neatly starched white aprons!

Dat and the boys got dressed sooner and had gone to the barn to hitch the horses to the buggies while the rest of us were getting ready. *Dat* was then waiting at the end of the sidewalk with Bud and Pearl, the old faithful team of brown buggy horses, hitched to the open surrey. Since there were not enough seats on the surrey to hold all twelve of us, the three oldest took the single seated buggy. Since I was the third born, I had the privilege of riding with Jerry and Al ma in Jerry's own shiny buggy, powered by his horse, Lady.

The ride to church was soon over since it was only a few miles. Upon arrival, we saw many people had already gathered there. Jerry dropped us off at the house, where the ladies, young girls, and small children were gathering. Alma and I placed our bonnets in the designated place on the enclosed porch. Joining the other teenage girls who were standing on the porch, we greeted each one with a customary handshake. I stood next to Katie as we waited quietly and reverently until it was time to take our seats.

Meanwhile, Jerry took his horse to the barn, where the men and young boys were gathering. The married men customarily greeted each other with the holy kiss. The unmarried members were greeted with a handshake only. This was also the custom for the married ladies and young girls. I was thankful the holy kiss was practiced only among the married members of like gender! Generally, at church only the preachers greeted those of the opposite gender, doing so with a handshake.

Shortly before nine o'clock, Bishop Eicher led the group of men and boys to the big, empty buggy shed. It was filled with dozens of homemade, backless, wooden benches, which had been arranged in neat rows the day before. With the big shed doors wide open, the gentle breeze gave some pleasant relief from the sultry summer heat. It was a welcome change from the crowded and humid conditions in the houses where services were normally held. By then, the women and small children were already seated on one side of the shed, while the men seated themselves on the opposite side facing the women. The teenage girls enjoyed sitting by themselves behind the ladies, while the teen boys were seated behind the married men.

After Bishop Eicher called the service to order, the congregation began singing from the German *Ausbund* in a drawn-out, monotone style. All the singing was done without accompaniment or parts of harmony. One song would require almost twenty minutes to be sung in its entirety. Bishop Eicher, along with his team of two assistant ministers, a deacon, and any visiting ministers, filed into the house to a private room for a counseling session. This was also when they planned the day's preaching schedule.

It was time for our baptismal group to follow them to the counseling room for the last instruction class of the summer. We had already had eight classes so far throughout the summer. We received another thirty or forty minutes of counseling from the ministers and reviewed the Articles of

Faith. We had also met at Bishop Eicher's home the day before to thoroughly review the baptismal Scriptures and Articles of Faith.

During the entire summer, the baptismal candidates were carefully observed and scrutinized by the ministers and church members. Misbehavior or violation of the church *Ordnung* could delay, or even prevent, one from being baptized. When a female baptismal candidate displayed a spirit of rebellion, such as wearing her dress too short or having her head covering shaped too neatly, or any other offense, she was considered not ready for baptism. It was evident that she was not willing to abide by the church *Ordnung,* and consequently not ready to be a member. Likewise, if the boys in the baptismal class shaved or trimmed their beard, or had their hat rim rolled up, or any other violation, it was considered an indication that they were not yet willing to support the church. It was mandatory that the candidates demonstrate a submissive spirit to the church *Ordnung* before baptism took place. Frequently, there were those clever ones who could display a compliant spirit in public, while they enjoyed doing as they pleased in secret. Their motto must have been, "What the preachers don't know can't hurt us!"

Somehow, all five of us convinced the Bishop and the church that we were ready to join the family of God, and the church, by baptism. The seventh Article of Faith states, *"...All penitent believers must be baptized with water in the most worthy name of the Father, Son, and Holy Spirit, to the burying of their sins and thus be incorporated into the fellowship of the saints."*

In addition to being reminded that Christ died for the sins of all mankind, we were carefully instructed that loyalty to the church *Ordnung* and traditions of our forefathers was supreme. That was how we were to avoid losing our church membership, without which we would most certainly lose all hope of eternal life. Such loyalty was also considered evidence that we had a desire to please God.

After being dismissed from class, we joined the rest of the congregation in singing the last hymn before the preaching began. We did not get to sit with the other young people as before. All five of us were seated on a bench prepared for us at the front of the room, facing the ministers' bench. The ministers were to be seated along the front wall, facing the congregation. The singing continued while we waited for the ministers to return to the bench in front of us.

I was in deep thought, as I realized that in my attempt to live a good life that would be pleasing to God, I had not always achieved that goal. I was eager to have my past sins washed away by the water of baptism, and get a new and clean start again. But only God knew that not until many years later would I be introduced to Someone who could truly lift my burden of sin, *set my feet upon a rock, and establish my goings.* (Palm 40:2b).

The singing stopped as the ministers rejoined the congregation. The first minister stood to preach for thirty minutes or more in our German dialect in the usual singsong fashion. Amazingly, he could touch on many different subjects in thirty minutes, without a Bible or sermon outline in hand. Many of the ministers had favorite passages and quotes memorized, which they recited every time it was their turn to preach.

An occasional trip to the outhouse by a mother with a young child or two in tow, or a baby's cry, would frequently divert one's attention from the preaching. There was no nursery provided. During the three-hour service, even the not-so-young would find relief for tired backs and legs by making a trip to the outhouse, whether nature called for it or not. Of course, for the men it was a trip to the barn.

When the preacher considered his duty accomplished, having preached from memory on a variety of subjects, he asked the congregation to kneel in prayer. Everyone turned around and knelt on the hard floor, facing the bench upon which they had been seated. The preacher read from the German prayer book for approximately ten minutes. During this long and tiresome kneeling, some listened to his reading while others fell asleep. Some mothers struggled to keep miserable babies and toddlers quiet. It was always a blessing when the minister could read quickly, which shortened the time in the uncomfortable position.

When the congregation stood again, a deacon read a chapter from the assigned Scriptures for the day. While this was an opportunity to stretch one's legs, some also made a quick trip to the outhouse or barn while the Scriptures were being read. Oddly enough, that seemed to be an accepted custom, provided one returned before the preaching resumed. Occasionally, a few young people who had stayed outside a bit too long would quickly find their way back to their seats just as the congregation was being seated again. Experience had taught them that staying outside much longer could bring a rebuke from the church elders.

At last, it was Bishop Eicher's turn to preach. He preached for forty-five minutes in a manner similar to the first preacher, without the singsong style. We looked forward to this time since one of his distinct gifts was to quote a great number of Scriptures and rehearse many interesting stories of the Old Testament saints, all from his amazingly keen memory.

The Greater Inheritance

The service had now been in session for a couple of hours. In spite of his interesting message, I began struggling with the temptation to let my weary eyes rest. I found temporary relief by adjusting my position on the hard, backless bench, as beads of perspiration trickled down my back. Being seated up front, under watchful eyes, I knew my wisest choice was to listen attentively and make every effort to stay awake.

Since I was a baptismal candidate, leaving the room for any reason was not a wise choice either. I took a quick glance around the room and realized I was not the only one struggling to keep my eyes open. Throughout the crowd, heads were nodding as others lost the battle to stay awake.

At last, the three-hour service was coming to a close. Bishop Eicher reached the point in the service in which he asked us to assume the proper position for baptism. We knelt in front of our bench, facing the ministers in front of us. I was getting very nervous and extremely uncomfortable as the whole congregation focused their attention on us. As young people, we were used to being seen and not heard. How could I possibly speak a few words aloud in front of the whole church? The very thought nearly petrified me.

Bishop Eicher then asked us the traditional questions, the first being, "Can you also confess with the eunuch, *'Yes, I believe that Jesus Christ is the Son of God?'* " To this, all five of us answered in turn, *Ja, ich glaube das Jesus Christus Gottes sohn isht* (Yes, I believe that Jesus Christ is the Son of God). I was relieved that the longest answer was completed.

The second question was, "Do you also recognize this to be a Christian order (or *Ordnung*), church, and fellowship under which you now submit yourselves?" Our answer of course was, *Ya* (Yes).

Third, we were asked, "Do you renounce the world, the devil with all his subtle ways, as well as your own flesh and blood, and desire to serve Jesus Christ alone, who died on the cross for you?" Again, we answered, *Ya.*

Last, but not least, we were asked, "Do you also promise before God and His church that you will support these teachings and regulations [church *Ordnung*] with the Lord's help, faithfully attend the services of the church and help to counsel and work in it, and not forsake it, whether it leads you to life or to death?"

While not realizing that this question was contrary to the third question of serving Jesus Christ alone, I once more answered, *Ya.* In fact, there was no other option. To do otherwise meant being denied church membership and losing all hope of eternal life, according to the Amish teachings. In addition, family and friends would treat that one as a rebel, whom they would not peacefully tolerate among their group. One then has only two choices: either join, or leave the church.

After receiving a satisfactory response to each question, Mrs. Eicher, the bishop's wife, removed my head covering. Bishop Eicher then began to perform his duty by cupping his hands over Ernest's head first, since he was the oldest. The deacon then dipped a tin cup into a small bucket of lukewarm water and slowly poured it into the bishop's hands, the water running down over the young man's head. I was the last one in line, since it is "gentlemen first" in the Amish culture. *At last my sins are about to be washed away,* I thought.

I barely heard the bishop say, "Upon your faith which you have confessed before God and many witnesses, you are baptized in the name of the Father, and the Son, and the Holy Spirit, Amen." The water ran down over my head and clothes, soaking wherever it went.

I was trembling uncontrollably from head to toe, causing great embarrassment to myself. Why public attention made me so extremely nervous, I did not understand. The other applicants appeared to be reasonably comfortable under the circumstances.

Mrs. Eicher replaced my head covering. The bishop then returned to the first one in line to extend his hand of welcome into the church family. He helped each one to their feet with the traditional phrase, " In the name of the Lord and the church, my hand is extended to you; stand up," and finished with the holy kiss. I was given a hand of welcome in the same manner, except for the holy kiss from Mrs. Eicher. That was a little unnerving as well.

After a dismissal hymn, I followed the other girls outside to the back yard. I had calmed down by then and felt greatly relieved that the whole ordeal was over.

We sat on benches under the shade tree and visited while we waited for the lady of the home and her relatives to prepare lunch in the house. The traditional church lunch consisted of bread, peanut butter, apple butter, strawberry jam, pickles, pickled beets, coffee, and tea. If church was at a well-to-do home, we could possibly expect sliced cheese, and even bologna at times.

I could hardly grasp the reality of now being a church member. Wow! What a milestone! I felt so clean, and almost holy. *If only I could keep my soul clean and my heart pure from now on,* I thought wistfully. But I knew the devil would not leave me alone for any length of time. He is always looking for his next "victim." All I wanted was to know that God was pleased with my life and would allow me into heaven someday. I concluded that I would just have to try my best to be a good church member by obeying the church *Ordnung*, as I had been taught, and surely, His grace would be sufficient where I lacked.

I did not attend the young people's singing in the evening. The custom for those having just been baptized was to stay at home that evening and meditate on the seriousness of their new position as a church member and their relationship with Christ. I was glad, in a sense, to stay at home. I reasoned that surely there would be less danger of corrupting my clean soul if I stayed at home with my parents and younger siblings.

Did You Know…

✓ A few Amish churches in less conservative communities have now started holding their services in a meeting house instead of in private homes. I am not aware of their reason for the change.

✓ The early New Testament church's social custom of greeting with the holy kiss is taught as a commandment of the Lord in numerous, but not all, Amish communities.

✓ The Amish never have Sunday evening church services or mid-week services; they meet for church only on Sunday mornings every two weeks. A few have Sunday School on alternate Sundays.

Chapter Eight

Questioning

I was a church member for only a short time when I became keenly aware of the fact that some families did not consider loyal conformity to the church *Ordnung* a top priority. Some members insisted on implementing a compromise of certain aspects of the clothing *Ordnung,* without the consent of the church. By all appearance, they were allowed to escape the consequences of their disobedience most of the time. Such violations were acceptable to only some of the church leaders, often resulting in contention among the members. That was extremely difficult for me to understand. *Are those "fence-crowders" not concerned about their eternal destiny? Do they expect to get to heaven in spite of their noncompliance to the church Ordnung?* I wondered.

Believing that unconditional conformity to the church *Ordnung* was a part of earning eternal life did not keep me from envying the "rebellious" ones, at times. I longed to experience the "freedom" they apparently enjoyed, such as relaxing our precise adherence to the clothing *Ordnung* in order to be more socially acceptable. Yet, I could not comprehend the possibility of living such a life without a tormenting guilt gnawing away in my well-trained Amish conscience.

Even so, the desire to fit in with the crowd became overwhelming at times. Consequently, my siblings and I frequently pleaded with my parents to make an exception to the clothing *Ordnung*. "Others do, why can we not, just once?" we questioned time after time. But the results of our pleadings were consistently negative, in our opinion. My parents always insisted that we live in flawless compliance to all of the church *Ordnungs* without exception. Our family was one of, if not the most, strict ones in the community. After all, if that was a factor in determining our eternal destiny, why take any risks of being found lacking in righteousness on Judgment Day? Who would not want to hear, "Well done, thou good and faithful servant?"

We were definitely in the minority. Not surprisingly, we experienced much ridicule and rejection from some of our peers, who considered our stand socially unacceptable. They had no use for such "grannies," or "black sheep," or whatever name they could come up with for us. Still, we were gratefully blessed with a small group of loyal friends who were moderately compliant with the *Ordnung* and accepted us in spite of our differences. They also endured some unpleasant experiences from the "elite" crowd.

At the time, I did not perceive it as God's mercy and blessing in disguise in protecting me from popularity with the crowd. Numerous times, our little group was spared from the consequences of their misbehavior, since we were not "one of them."

We were taught that helping another conceal his sins makes us partakers of it as well. Thus, for conscience sake, any knowledge of another's hidden wrongdoings had to be reported to the ministers. Yet none of us wanted to report

The Greater Inheritance

them for fear of retaliation from the erring ones, such as verbal abuse, spiteful name-calling, or even destruction of property. As a precaution, the group who enjoyed the pleasure of their forbidden possessions in secret did not consider our friendship trustworthy. They were not willing to be put at risk of having to give up their radios, cigarettes, and booze, or any other violations they decided to engage in. Ignorance was bliss for us in those circumstances!

Only years later did God allow me to understand, at least in part, that He had a definite purpose in allowing me to experience each of those trials in my youth. I shall be forever grateful to Him for protecting me from social popularity. He knew it would have been a hindrance to His plans for my future. One hymn-writer says, *God never moves without purpose or plan.* I am also reminded of Genesis 50:20, *Ye thought evil against me; but God meant it unto good.*

Unable to change our financial and social status in life, my siblings and I chose to rise above the circumstances, appreciate the small group of wonderful friends we had, and enjoy life as much as possible.

John and I had been dating frequently for almost a year when he felt the need to put our relationship on hold for a time in order to sort through some personal and spiritual turmoil. Although I knew he still cared about our friendship, it was a trying time for me. I did not know how to trust God that He would accomplish His will in His own timing. Admittedly, I habitually agonized and worried about the future of our relationship. *How could it not be His will?* I wondered repeatedly.

Helplessly, I felt my only option was to hope and pray, and then hope some more. I was not familiar with praying without a book, but I developed my own prayer concerning our future. I prayed almost daily that God would bring us back together. I was not sure He would listen to me, or even cared about such things, but I did not think it would hurt to try. Somehow life continued.

During the time John and I had discontinued dating, my friend Katie and her brother Enos frequently provided me with transportation to and from the singings. We had much enjoyment together on those sometimes-lengthy Sunday evening rides. There was never a dull moment around Katie! Although she had a mischievous side, her good-natured and kind personality had a tendency to draw others to her. My intent was to enjoy our friendship as much as possible, without getting involved in the "mischief" in which she seemed to find herself frequently! I succeeded most of the time, knowing my parents would immediately terminate our friendship if I let them down. That would not have been a pleasant day for any of us.

The following spring, I helped *Dat* and my brothers farm the one hundred sixty acres of land *Dat* owned. One of them would harness five husky workhorses for me to hitch to the gangplow. For the next several weeks, I spent many days in the sun as I guided the horses, round after round, across the field. No doubt, I enjoyed the occasional break at the end of the field as much as the horses did. While they rested their tired muscles and regained their strength for yet another round, I could hasten to the water jug under the shade tree. I enjoyed the smell of freshly turned earth, although my favorite job in the field was raking hay.

I mostly enjoyed the time alone to think about my future, wondering what God had planned for me. Hoping and praying had become a major part of my daily thought life throughout the summer.

Once again, summer quickly turned to fall. Soon the hustle and bustle of preparing for the cold winter ahead divided my thoughts between the present and the future.

It was the time of year to take the teams and wagons and head to the cornfield. Many acres of corn needed to be harvested by hand before the snow fell.

Jerry had moved out of the house by now, although he was not married yet. That left only Ervin and John to help *Dat* with the harvesting. The custom was that all the available women in the house helped with the corn harvest. Alma and I got to work alongside *Dat,* each shucking one row, while he took two rows at a time. Even then, we had to hurry to keep up with him. It helped to have Lovina tagging along to pick up the ears that occasionally missed the wagon.

If given the choice, I would have chosen any other work on the farm over shucking corn. It was just not my favorite fieldwork. On the other hand, listening to *Dat's* stories from his younger years as we tossed one ear of corn after another into the wagon made a monotonous task seem a bit more pleasant. The continuous "bang-bang-bang" of ears of corn hitting the wagon soon turned into a contest. Ervin and John, along with Rachel, had the other team and wagon several rows over and were trying to get to the end of their rows before we finished ours. They had Anna along to pick up their stray ears of corn.

By lunchtime, we had worked up a voracious appetite. No time was wasted in unhitching the horses and putting them in the barn to munch down their lunch. We all dragged our exhausted bodies to the house for a hearty country-style meal. *Mem,* Lizzie, and Sadie had prepared a delicious feast on the old wood-burning range in the kitchen. Steaming bowls of homegrown vegetables, mashed potatoes, gravy, and meat were set before us, as we promptly found our usual place at the old, wobbly dining table.

If we were fortunate, *Mem* would surprise us with some delicious pies for dessert, although that was a rare occurrence. We very seldom had pies unless company was at the table. Even then, we often had only mixed fruit for dessert, and *Mem* would declare her all-time most famous words,—*Longets brote vidda rum; mia hen ken kucha otta boy* (Pass the bread again; we don't have any cake or pie).

After we had stuffed our stomachs to near gluttony, everyone was allowed a brief rest before returning to work. Shortly, *Dat* and the boys had the ears of corn unloaded into the corn bin with the grain shovels, and it was time to head back to the field.

Once we were back in the cornfield, the banging of the ears flying into the wagons resumed with renewed vigor. We were soon calculating how many weeks it would take to harvest the whole field. The results were not exactly thrilling. Obviously, the weather was a major factor.

After a while, the mind-numbing task of harvesting each of the hundreds of thousands of ears of corn in that big field, one at a time by hand, provoked some questions in my mind. Eventually I summoned the courage to ask *Dat* why our church would not allow the use of the horse-drawn corn pickers, similar to the ones used in some other Amish communities. "Is it not poor stewardship of our time to use this method when pickers could accomplish the same task in much less time?" I ventured to ask.

As usual, *Dat* paused a while before responding. He had the wonderful characteristic of thinking before he spoke. He reminded me that it was the guideline in our community to keep to traditional methods, so that was the way it had to be done. Obviously, he meant that the church leaders and members agreed to prohibit corn pickers, considering them too modern. Since our particular church prohibited it, getting a corn picker would have been considered sin and rebellion, earning us a reputation with consequences that any loyal member would not want to face. Apparently, there was no definite scriptural explanation for the restriction; it was simply an effort to stay with traditions and keep our distance from the worldly culture by avoiding modern conveniences.

I knew my only option was to accept that philosophy and continue plucking away on those boring ears of corn, day after day, until the whole thirty to forty acres of corn were finished.

Did You Know…

✓ Although the goal of all Amish churches is to keep all their members within the prescribed boundaries of fellowship, an increasing number choose to question the validity of the restrictions placed upon them. Some who leave look for the answers in the Scriptures, while others rebel against all religion, apparently as a result of their strict upbringing.

The Greater Inheritance

Chapter Nine

Dawning of Truth

*I*n spite of not finishing the corn harvest before Christmas that year, it was the most wonderful Christmas ever for a very special reason!

On that Christmas Sunday in 1977, we went to church as usual. In the evening we went back for supper and singing. As far as I was concerned, it was just another routine Sunday evening.

However, to my astonishment, after the singing was over, John sent a young man to ask my permission to take me home again. I nearly gasped with delight. John and I had not had any communication with each other for about a year and a half. I did not know what he had in mind by then concerning our relationship. My hope and optimism had begun to dim, and I wondered if I would ever hear those words. My soul was overwhelmed with joy! *Maybe God does hear prayers, even mine!* I thought. We had a wonderful evening getting reacquainted! My family rejoiced with me the next day when I informed them of who had brought me home the night before.

John and I dated every two weeks for a while. Our relationship soon progressed to a weekly date, with us being allowed to see each other only on Sunday evenings, or once a week. How I looked forward to those Sunday evenings when he would bring me home from the singing and we would have the privilege of seeing each other again!

As life moved me ever onward, the months and years ahead were not always easy. It was especially difficult when I compared our unflattering dress standards with those of some other communities. They looked much neater than we did, yet appeared perfectly modest and godly in dress. I could not understand why our unsightly "one-inch-wide apron band" rule was godlier than a "two-inch band" rule allowed in other communities. Nor why having my apron four inches shorter than my dress was better than having it the same length. We were one of the two or three families in the whole community who gave heed to those two specific *Ordnungs*. Apparently most of the church leaders chose not to enforce them, as their own wives and daughters ignored those rules. Not so in my *mem's* house; if it was said once, it was an inflexible "law" in her books!

The width of the head covering strings was another issue of frequent contentions. Some desired one-fourth-inch-wide strings, while others presumed one-half-inch-wide strings to be more humble. It was supposedly less worldly for the men's shirts to have no more than three front buttons. Likewise, for men to hold their trousers in place with suspenders over their shoulders was deemed better than wearing a belt around the waist as the "world" does. For every item of clothing we made, except underwear, we had guidelines to follow, requiring much measuring and close attention to detail, color, and texture of the fabrics used.

Yes, it was the regulation in our community. And yes, I agreed to follow it when I was baptized. However, there were apparently no scriptural grounds for the specific

The Greater Inheritance

guidelines. Obviously, it was merely what the church considered the best strategy to keep its members within certain boundaries. That often resulted in destructive bickering among the members. Of course, the only peaceful option for those who disagreed with certain aspects of the *Ordnung* was to move to another community of their own choice, or establish a new community, instituting the rules they preferred.

I comforted myself with the thought of possibly someday getting married and moving to a community where the church's *Ordnung* seemed a bit more reasonable. Logically, that would also have meant experiencing less strife. However, I assumed we must be certain that it was a church under the Amish "umbrella," representing a religion guided by a precise *Ordnung* and traditions. Given that they all function under the same basic system, to various degrees, I concluded we would still be sheltered from the worldly culture, no matter which Amish community we joined.

Although I felt a tinge of guilt while entertaining such thoughts, I enjoyed imagining a better future. Confusion and uncertainty had become a normal part of life. Apparently, the only answer at times was to accept that some situations in life simply demanded conformity, without valid grounds of justification. I am thankful that God knew my sincere desire to make some sense of it all. He showed me that He knows the heart of every individual when He sent an "English" friend across my path several years later who knew exactly what the need of every individual is.

It was in the fall of 1979 when Ervin met *Mr. Harrison*, an "English" gentleman who later became a chauffeur for the Amish people. *Mr. Harrison* was simply carrying out his Christian responsibility of telling others about the Savior when he began to share the Bible with Ervin. Soon after that Glen Yoder and his wife Ida also met *Mr. Harrison* and cautiously listened to the scriptures he shared with them. Ervin and Glen began to realize that the teachings they were hearing from him were straight from God's Word. They eventually shared those truths with me, my brother John and his friend Mattie. Although John, my husband-to-be, was interested and knew about it, he did not have an opportunity to become involved very much until later.

Our small group soon learned enough truth to realize there was much more that we needed to know. *Mr. Harrison* gave us some sermon tapes to listen to, along with a tape player, which obviously was not in accordance with the church *Ordnung*. Our desire for truth overruled, and we enjoyed learning about the Bible through these tapes, although it had to be done strictly in secret. Our motives were not of rebellion against the church whatsoever, but of a sincere desire to find answers to our questions.

In order to keep from being prohibited to continue our studies, we had no choice but to find a hiding place where our group could listen to the encouraging messages of God's Word.

One such hiding place was at Mattie's home after dark. She was the last of their children still living at home, and her parents were on vacation at the time. We locked all their doors, except the one that would not lock. That door we secured by pushing a big galvanized tub against it, which would create a loud noise should someone try to enter. We could not afford to let anyone drop in on us accidentally. When we felt comfortably safe, someone grabbed a flashlight, and we all hurried to a dark upstairs bedroom.

There we huddled around the tape player, turning it just loud enough to be heard up close.

After enjoying those meetings at various hideouts for several months, our secret suddenly was at great risk of being exposed to the public. The horrifying episode took place at a friend's house one Sunday evening after the singing. That was where our meetings were held occasionally. Our friend was gone for the weekend, leaving Ervin in charge. I stayed there for the night as well. Shortly before I retired for the night, I heard a strange disturbance in the back of the house. With alarm I realized it was not Ervin coming home from his date. Judging by the commotion I heard, I realized it was a group of intruders, who were swiftly rummaging through the closet and a dresser in a back bedroom. I was petrified when I remembered that Ervin had hidden the tape player in that room.

While I suspected the intruders were Amish teenage boys, and did not believe I was in danger of personal harm, I was not brave enough to confront them. The next eight to ten minutes seemed like an hour as I waited nervously. When there were no more sounds coming from the bedroom, I assumed they were gone.

Cautiously, I opened the door to survey the damage. The intruders had entered through a back door and then ransacked the bedroom by rummaging through drawers and the closet, leaving items scattered across the floor. The tape player appeared to be undisturbed, although we were not certain that it had gone undetected.

Later, we learned who a few of the vandals were, although we never learned what motivated the raid. Apparently, they were simply doing what unregenerate young people do naturally—find pleasure and entertainment in all the wrong places.

After we reported the raid to the Bishop, the main culprits' sentence was to deliver an apology to us. That closed the case as far as they were concerned. Yet, we were disturbed by the possibility that our secret had been discovered. If they had found the tape player, we realized we were in serious trouble with the church. The tape player would be confiscated, and we would be facing church discipline, if not excommunication. By no means did we want to give the impression that we were a group of rebels.

Our small group decided the best choice was to dispose of the tape player before it caused any public disgrace. Ervin promptly took care of it—how, I do not know. As far as we were concerned, it was gone. Our meetings were less frequent for a while, and things quieted down somewhat for all of us. Nevertheless, the truths we had learned from the Bible were safely tucked away deep within our hearts, waiting to take root and grow. God knew our hearts' desire, and in His own timing, He would provide nourishment for those roots to spring forth and accomplish His plan.

Did You Know...

✓ Seldom will the Amish call the authorities on anyone for any reason, especially not on their own people. The church takes care of any offenses committed by the church members. Neither do the Amish participate in the political voting and election process.

✓ All Amish practice a religion of nonresistance. They oppose wars and government interference in their lives. They believe killing in self-defense is murder. Their presumption is that if all people would live as the Amish do, there would be no wars and no need for big government.

✓ Most Amish churches have an *Ordnung* letter, which is an established set of rules written by the Bishop and preachers. Therein are the descriptions of the specific measurements, styles, colors, and textures description of clothing that the church allows, or requires, its members to wear. That includes every piece of visible clothing from the hat or bonnet to the socks, shoes, and boots. In addition, the types of farm machinery, buggies, and any motor-powered equipment must fall under certain guidelines. Basically, every aspect of an Amish person's life is under the control of the church.

The Greater Inheritance

Chapter Ten

Wedding

*M*onths turned to years, and by Christmas of 1979, John and I had been dating again for two years. Our plans for an early spring wedding were well underway. No one was aware of our secret plans yet, except our parents and older siblings. The engagement and wedding date were traditionally kept secret until two or three weeks before the wedding. The engagement, or *ausgerufa,* would then be announced publicly to the church. We eagerly anticipated that day when it would no longer need to be kept secret and others could rejoice with us.

In the meantime, there was a buzz of activity taking place at home while we tried to avoid all suspicion by the public. Since Amish wedding dinners are held at the bride's home, there was not only much cleaning to do, but also a list of clothing items to sew. My sisters and I were kept busy sewing new dresses for each one of us and for *Mem.* Then there were white shirts to make for *Dat* and my brothers. We managed to get most of the sewing completed in secrecy before our engagement.

At last, it was the day of our engagement! Following the closing hymn after the church service, the Bishop announced our plans of getting married. We could now freely prepare for our wedding day. No more hiding the evidence in case a visitor dropped in. What a relief that was!

The next day, for the first time ever, John and I were allowed to go to town by ourselves. I could hardly believe it was really happening: it was our own wedding for which we were buying. We bought all the necessary grocery items we could get in advance in preparation for the wedding, considering that we had no refrigeration available. Refrigerators were not allowed in our community.

John was then allowed to stay with my family most of the next two weeks until the wedding day to help with the work. There was the yard to manicure, and all the outbuildings to clean up. I was thankful the men took care of most of the outside work, including preparing the barn for the many horses the guests would be driving to our wedding.

The womenfolk spent that time cleaning and scrubbing the house, taking care of food preparations, and tending to the many other details involved. Every room and closet in the house had to be thoroughly cleaned, from the floor to the ceiling. The twenty-four windows could not be ignored either. Customarily, everything had to be sparkling clean. My parents were situated better financially by then and were able to purchase some paint for a few rooms that were begging for it.

Almost a week in advance, the tables were set up banquet style in the living room, kitchen, and main bedroom. Most of the furniture was moved out and stored in the spare bedroom upstairs and in outbuildings. Tables were set up in the basement as well. After all the tables were set with the appropriate tableware, they were covered with sheets to protect them until the day of the wedding. John and I had the privilege of working together preparing the tables and doing various other projects.

The level of anticipation was rising every day! It was the first time the exciting wedding preparations were for someone in our family.

We borrowed many china plates, cups, serving bowls, lots of silverware, big pots and pans, and various other items from relatives and neighbors. Then there were also dozens of chickens to butcher, besides baking approximately forty pies of three different varieties, along with thirty to thirty-five three-layer cakes. All the cake icings were homemade as well.

All the sisters, in-laws, aunts, my *Grosmommy,* and any close female relatives of the bride and groom who lived in the community came to help with the food preparations on the last few days.

The day before the wedding was filled with preparing fruit salads, puddings, and ingredients for potato salad. That was also when I put the final touches on the bridal cake, which was about twelve inches high and twelve inches in diameter. I covered it with white homemade frosting and then sprinkled it with shredded coconut on the top and sides, accenting the top with pecan halves. We were not allowed to decorate the cake or the rooms with flowers or any kind of décor.

After supper, some relatives started arriving from out of state. They spent the night at the neighbors' and relatives' homes close by. The two couples who were to be our attendants also arrived for the night, because they needed to be there early the next morning.

By bedtime, *Mem* and I had checked and double-checked to ensure all preparations were in place, hoping to prevent any unforeseeable embarrassing moments the next day. At last, I slipped under the covers just before midnight. I attempted to relax my racing mind before drifting off on a short dreamland journey. Everyone else was already several miles down that road.

Four o'clock came quickly, and the merciless blaring of the alarm clock rudely awakened me. Fumbling for the object of disturbance on my nightstand, I was suddenly jerked to reality. That noise indicated it was March 25, 1980, our wedding day at last! It was also my twenty-second birthday, making the day even a bit more special.

The clear twinkling sky was promising a perfect day for a wedding. I sensed that it was going to be the happiest day of my life!

Dat and the boys did the milking that morning. I had many other things to tend to and was thankful to be relieved from outside responsibilities.

After a quick breakfast, we dashed upstairs to get dressed in our traditional wedding clothes. I wore my new navy dress with a starched sheer white apron and shoulder cape over it, along with a black head covering. The two girls who were to be our attendants wore the same colors and styles.

John and the two male attendants wore their white shirts and navy suits. The attendants are traditionally two couples closely related to, or close friends of, the bride and groom. We chose to have my brother Ervin and his girlfriend Elizabeth, who was also John's sister, as one couple. My sister Alma and her friend *Herman* were the other set of attendants.

At seven o'clock, the three *hostlers* (chauffeurs) were there to transport the wedding party to our neighbor's house, where the wedding service was to be held. It was after seven-thirty by the time we were situated at the neighbors. They had a special place prepared for us in the dining room, where the ladies would also be seated later.

Soon several hundred guests were arriving in a steady stream. After many had come by to greet us and were seated in their proper places, the service began at nine o'clock.

As the first traditional wedding song began, Bishop Eicher and six to eight ministers filed upstairs to the counseling room. John and I were to join them for about thirty minutes of counseling regarding the marriage Scriptures. Equally important were the teachings and readings recited from the book of Tobit, in *The Apocrypha,* a book used in addition to the Bible. It is the historical and fictional writings of men, apart from divine inspiration.

That counseling session was essentially the extent of marriage counseling we received from anyone in preparation for marriage. For most Amish couples entering into marriage, "live and learn" is not merely a cliché, but a reality. Some matters were considered too personal to discuss, and other common married life issues were not considered necessary counseling topics. Allegedly, the young couple was equipped to enter into marriage by observing their parents' life. When problems would rear their ugly head—well, they would just have to learn how to deal with those difficulties then.

After we were dismissed from the counseling room upstairs, we again joined the rest of the congregation. We were then ceremoniously seated with our attendants at the front of the living room, close to the ministers' bench. We had ample time to seize the moment as another song was sung while we waited for the ministers to return. I glanced at John, wishing I could read his mind as we sat in solemn meditation. I wondered if the minutes seemed like hours to him as well, as we eagerly waited for the preachers to continue with the rest of the service.

When the singing ended, the first preacher stood to preach, similar to a typical church service. He preached on various subjects, some not particularly related to the occasion. In closing his portion of the service, the congregation knelt as he read a prayer. Since we had asked Bishop Yoder to perform the vows, he preached for the last forty-five minutes of the service.

After a while, it was almost twelve o'clock, and time for us to be joined in holy matrimony. That sacred moment was about to become reality!

The cooks and table waiters had arrived in time to witness the exchange of the vows. The whole congregation was eager to see them come in, and discover which young people were teamed up to wait on tables. Some were courting couples, while others were matched up only for the day. The helpers were not revealed to the general public until then.

At Bishop Yoder's request, John and I nervously stepped forward and stood before him to repeat the vows. He joined our hands as we promised to remain faithful to each other "until death do us part." Kissing the bride publicly was not a part of the Amish tradition. There were no rings to exchange either, because wearing jewelry was perceived to be a worldly practice. However, we were married nonetheless.

As we returned to our seats, I tried to grasp the reality of us now being husband and wife. What a blessed milestone we had reached! Amazingly, God gave me a husband of remarkable character, who deserved my very best as his helpmeet, by God's grace.

The closing hymn was sung and the wedding party was dismissed first. The cooks and helpers had already left, immediately after the vows were exchanged.

The same three *hostlers* who had brought us to the service were waiting again with their buggies in the front of the house, to transport our attendants and us to the wedding feast in my parents' home. We noticed the pleasantly warm and sunny day as we rode along. The rest of the congregation followed shortly.

The delicious aroma of food welcomed us as we entered the dining area. There was a flurry of activity as the twenty-five designated cooks, consisting of both of our *mems,* our aunts, John's sisters, and sisters-in-law, tended to their designated jobs. They had been working diligently since eight o'clock that morning, preparing mashed potatoes, gravy, baked chicken, dressing, noodles, and vegetables. Meanwhile, the six sets of table waiters and three additional single waitresses were scurrying about, filling serving bowls with potato salad, fruit salads, and puddings. They also had to cut the thirty-five cakes and forty pies, in addition to serving coffee.

John and I and our attendants were seated at our own special section of the main table, set with fancy dinnerware and special dishes. Soon the first shift of a hundred and fifty guests were seated at the tables. Dozens of bowls of steaming food were delivered by the table waiters as they served their designated tables. The remaining guests enjoyed a time of visiting while they patiently waited until the second shift to eat. There were still fifty to seventy-five guests to serve.

After everyone had had their fill, big bowls of many varieties of candy bars were passed around the tables for the guests before they left. That was a token of appreciation from the bride and groom to the guests for sharing the day with us. I remember that as a little girl that was the best part of the wedding as far as I was concerned! It was one of the few times I ever had the privilege of enjoying a candy bar.

The afternoon was spent singing various German hymns and visiting with relatives whom we had not seen in many years.

By late afternoon the majority of our local guests had left. The cooks had a short break before it was time for them to begin the process all over again in preparation for the evening meal. They had plates and silverware to wash before the tables could be reset. The evening meal was a full meal again, but with less variety.

We had invited all of our relatives and close neighbors, as well as the out-of-state guests to come back for the evening meal. That included many of our cousins, aunts, and uncles from Indiana. It was such a joy to have them share our special day with us. Many of them had never been to our house before.

Most of the young people of the community had also come back for the evening. They were allowed to sit with their dates for the evening meal. Even the married people were eager to see who was matched up with whom for the evening! That was usually prearranged when the young people gathered upstairs before being seated at the tables. If a young fellow wished to escort a certain girl to the table, he asked a friend to get her permission. Sometimes that was the beginning of a relationship that eventually led to yet another wedding.

After the meal, the young people sang German songs for about an hour. Those songs were not as slow and drawn out as the church hymns. Soon all the young people were leaving, some with their dates.

Before our waiters and cooks could leave, John and I had to be certain they each received a gift of appreciation for their day's work. All the cooks were given a gift basket of fresh fruit. We added a big slice of the bridal cake to it just before they left. The table waiter's customary gift was a parfait glass with a fancy handkerchief neatly folded and arranged around the outside of it, then filled with a variety of candy. We then placed a frosted and decorated "cured" cookie at an angle in the top of the parfait glass. The cookies had their names and the wedding date on it. They were not edible, but rather a keepsake. They also received some fresh fruit and a big slice of the bridal cake.

With all the major details of the day taken care of, the mountains of dirty dishes had to wait until the next day. Ervin, Elizabeth, *Herman,* and Alma stayed for the night, since one of their duties as attendants was to help wash the gigantic stacks of dishes, pots, and pans the next day.

Incredibly, our special day was ending quickly. We rejoiced in the blessed day it had been, rich with wonderful memories to hold in our hearts forever. There were no honeymoon trips for newlyweds in our community. Soon after midnight, when the entire wedding day was history, we finally retired for the night.

When John and I walked into our upstairs bedroom, we realized we could not retire just yet. It seemed our bed was groaning under a mountain of wedding gifts. We were very grateful for every one of them; however, they had to be moved to the corner of the room until morning.

Wednesday morning came incredibly soon. We were tempted to explore the gigantic mound of gifts over in the corner before we went down for breakfast, eager to see what we had received to set up house and begin our life together. But we resisted, as we remembered that we had a big task down in the kitchen waiting for our attention.

After breakfast, everyone helped us as we tackled the duty before us. Big tubs were used to soak the dishes that were stuck with dried food. We took turns washing and drying dishes by hand until every piece was spotless. With my new husband helping me, the job was rather enjoyable. I am sure Elizabeth and Alma found that working with their special friends made the job much more pleasant for them too. We all had a fun and enjoyable time working together, and finished up shortly before lunchtime.

The many borrowed plates, silverware, cups, serving bowls, pots, and pans were then ready to be returned to the owners. We spent the rest of the day cleaning up the house, and then Ervin took Elizabeth home. *Herman* was also free to go home then. By evening we were tired enough to appreciate a good night's rest.

Did You Know ...

✓ No matter how happily married, most married couples do not express any affection to each other publicly. Although some experience very difficult marriages, a divorce is not an option, even if it has taken place in the heart. They believe the biblical teaching of Mark 10:9, *What therefore God hath joined together, let not man put asunder.* They cannot legally divorce and remain a part of the Amish church.

Chapter Eleven

Life Together

*T*he following day, Thursday, was another memorable day for us. John and I packed our numerous wedding gifts and the few belongings I had accumulated in my twenty-two years at home. We loaded everything on my father-in-law's iron-wheeled, flatbed hay wagon. It had twelve-inch-high sideboards on it, keeping our belongings from falling off along the way. We hoped the glassware would survive the trip to our new home.

After lunch we climbed aboard and seated ourselves on the blanket-covered hay bale positioned at the front of the wagon. As we waved good-bye to my family, John took the reins in his hands and signaled the horses to begin the journey. With eager hearts, we drove off into our future, traveling the seven miles down a dusty gravel road to our temporary home. Only God, in His great omniscience, knew the trials we would face about four years from that time.

We arrived at John's parents' house before dark. His family helped unload our belongings into their biggest bedroom upstairs, which was to be our one-room home until our house was built. They still had their three youngest daughters, Elizabeth, Emma, and Rosa, at home.

Our lives soon settled into a daily routine, and John helped his *dat* run the family farm. We formed many pleasant memories while living with them. In retrospect, we realize we were obviously quite inexperienced as tenants, and sometimes too inconsiderate. Gratefully, we were allowed much grace and patience as both families adjusted to living in the same house.

In October of that year, Ervin and Elizabeth were married. We were still living in the upstairs with our new house near enough to completion to hold the wedding service in it.

A month after their wedding, we moved into our new house across the yard from the big family farmhouse. It was built with the intentions to someday serve as my in-laws' *dawdyhaus* (grandfather house, or retirement home). What a joy it was to move from a one-room home to a four-room house! We had two bedrooms, a living room, a kitchen/dining room, and a walk-in pantry, besides the unfinished upstairs. Although living upstairs in the big house had its own advantages, the move came just in time to allow us to have a blessed Thanksgiving Day indeed.

A few months after moving into our new house, we received another blessing when our first baby, a girl, was born at a hospital in a nearby town. We named her Rosa, after John's sister, with no middle name. Giving a middle name was considered to be starting the child off to a life of pride, according to most people's opinions in our very conservative community.

Emma and Rosa took turns coming over to help whenever I needed them. My sisters also helped occasionally. I cannot imagine what I would have done without each one of them. They helped me so much during the years we lived there, and I greatly appreciated them.

We have no baby photos of our little Rosa, since the church did not permit cameras and photos. The church believed the possession of photos to be a violation of the second commandment in Exodus 20:4, *Thou shalt not make unto thee any graven image, or any likeness of any thing that is in heaven above, or that is in the earth beneath, or that is in the water under the earth.* We now have come to understand that the next verse clarifies that this commandment is forbidding the making and worship of false gods, rather than the depiction of an object or an individual as a keepsake. Exodus 20:5 says, *Thou shalt not bow down thyself to them, nor serve them.*

Two years later in 1983, we were blessed with a healthy baby boy, born in the same hospital where we had little Rosa. We named him Omer, simply because we liked the name, but later unofficially changed the spelling to Omar. Once more, we had no baby pictures. The sisters willingly helped us again, whenever we needed them.

Soon it was gardening time again. I was quickly becoming a busy *mem* with the housework, gardening, and caring for our family.

John was busy helping his *dat* in the fields. After the corn was planted, putting up hay was in full swing. His married brothers came to help until all the hay was baled and neatly stacked in the hayloft. John then returned the help when their hay was ready to be put up.

Generally, after a couple had been married a year or more, they were expected to take their turn in hosting the church service at their house. We eventually took our turn having church services, which were held in the big house. Our house was too small to seat all the people. Nevertheless, our own house had to be thoroughly cleaned, since it would be used as a place of fellowship for some of the ladies after the service. On Thursday or Friday, the sisters and neighbors came to help clean and finish most of the major jobs. On Saturday, I baked the pies for the Sunday evening meal for the young people. Finishing up various small jobs and mopping the floor completed the day.

Did You Know ...

✓ When Amish children are not given a middle name, the first letter of their father's name becomes their middle initial. That identifies them with the family to which they belong.

✓ Over the years, with a change of church leadership in Bowling Green, many changes have slowly but certainly drifted into the church. Some of which are babies' middle names, and even non-traditional names occasionally. A more lenient dress *Ordnung* is also very evident there today. Many of these changes would certainly have resulted in severe church discipline twenty or twenty-five years ago. One must question their claim of keeping the traditions of their forefathers, and a scripture based *Ordnung*, given that God's Word never changes.

✓ The youngest son of the family is traditionally expected to take over the family farm after marriage or when the father comes to retirement age. At that time, the parents move into the *dawdyhaus*, and the son and his family occupy the bigger house.

John's childhood home

Our new house before Thanksgiving Day

The Greater Inheritance

Chapter Twelve

Ordnung Services

*C*ounsel meetings, or *Ordnung* services, were held once every spring and fall. They would begin, as usual, at nine o'clock, but then continue all day until four or five o'clock. Many did not look forward to that long day of sitting. It was especially tiring for the little children.

At lunchtime, the lady of the house and a few of her relatives left the service to prepare the usual church lunch in another part of the house. It may have been in a big washhouse or a large enclosed porch adjacent to the house. When the food was ready, a dozen or more people at a time left the room where the service was held to take their turn at the table, cafeteria style. Usually the elderly ate first. I was always relieved when it was my age group's turn to eat. Those twenty to thirty minutes were the longest break we would get all day. The service stayed in progress during all the lunch shifts. By one-thirty or two o'clock, everyone had finished lunch and the dishes were cleared away.

A few hours later, the children could all breathe a sigh of relief when it was time to dismiss them and the teens who were not members of the church yet. Most of them went home, while a few stayed as babysitters. Before I became a member, I always enjoyed staying to help care for the babies and toddlers while their parents sat through the "members only" session. Behind closed doors, with only the members present, it was time to rehearse the church *Ordnung.* Sometimes they would even add a few new ones. A general warning was given for those who were testing the boundaries too much, especially the young people.

Church discipline was administered during that time when necessary. Usually, the investigation was done beforehand, and the offender was required to confess his or her misdemeanor to the church, asking forgiveness from the church and God. I never understood why confessing it to God only was not sufficient in cases where He alone knew about the offense. The Bible tells us there is only *one mediator between God and men, the man Christ Jesus* (I Timothy 2:5). As we understand it now, James was not speaking of a public confession when he used the singular form saying, *Confess your faults one to another, and pray one for another, that ye may be healed* (James 5:16).

If the transgression, either private or public, was severe enough, such as possession a radio, drunkenness, or immorality, then there was no second chance. That person was excommunicated for four to six weeks. During that time, he could not eat with his own family and other church members, nor associate with others unless absolutely necessary. The seventeenth Article of Faith from the Dordrecht Confession of 1632, used to instruct baptismal candidates, says:

> *Concerning the withdrawing from or shunning of the separated, we believe and confess that when someone has fallen so far, either by his evil life or perverted doctrine, that he is severed from God and as a consequence justly separated and punished by the church, such a person must, according to*

The Greater Inheritance

the teaching of Christ and His apostles, also be shunned and avoided without partiality by all the fellow members of the church—in eating and drinking and other similar association,[2] thus having no dealings with him, lest by such contact one become defiled or partaker of his sins. Rather, that the sinner might be made ashamed, be stirred in his mind, and convicted in his conscience to repentance...accordingly, one should not consider them as enemies but admonish them as brethren in order to bring them to knowledge, repentance, and sorrow for their sins[3] so that they may be reconciled to God and His church, and consequently be received and taken in again. And that love toward them may continue as is fitting.

A banned person had to spend some time in the preachers' counseling room at every service until his or her sentence was terminated. His sentence was not fulfilled until the preachers judged him as being repentant. At that time, he had to make a public confession to the members at church, admitting that he had sinned and had deserved the punishment of being shunned. He was then reinstated as a member, to continue his life in peace again. I often felt a sense of relief for that one who could now return to a normal life with the rest of the family.

Communion service followed two weeks after the counsel meeting. The services were much alike, accept this time we observed the Lord's Supper and a foot-washing ceremony in the afternoon, instead of reviewing the

---

[2] I Corinthians 5:9-11; II Thessalonians 3:14; Titus 3:10

[3] II Thessalonians 3:14- *And if any man obey not our word by this epistle, note that man, and have no company with him, that he may be ashamed.*

Ordnung. For communion, unsalted homemade bread was used to represent Christ's body broken for our sins.

I often wondered how the deacon made the fermented wine we used to represent Christ's blood which He shed upon the cross for us. Customarily, the wine was served by the deacon in the service. The same cup was used for everyone, passing it from one member to another, and simply refilling it as needed.

After the Lord's Supper, during the closing hymn, the foot-washing ceremony was performed. The members took turns by twos, going to a designated area in the room to wash each other's feet in a foot tub. Of course, it was men with men, and women with women. The ceremony was concluded with the holy kiss between the two.

Our understanding of John 13 had always been that Jesus was speaking of literal foot washing. However, we now see that verse 7 of that chapter provides evidence contrary to that interpretation. *Jesus answered and said unto him, What I do thou knowest not now; but thou shalt know hereafter.* Evidently, He was illustrating a deeper issue. We believe Jesus was teaching humility and that we should humble ourselves before one another. The Bible also never indicates that any local church in the New Testament observed literal foot washing because of this incident. In verse 8, Jesus said to Peter, *If I wash thee not, thou hast no part with me.* We can be sure Jesus was not teaching His disciples that literal foot washing would make them one with Him spiritually. Otherwise, their salvation would be in part by their own deeds, which we know is not what the Bible teaches: *Not by works of righteousness which we have done, but according to his mercy he saved us, by the washing of regeneration, and renewing of the Holy Ghost* (Titus 3:5).

We have since learned there are only two ordinances that Christ has commanded the church to observe— baptism (Matthew 28:18-20) and the Lord's Supper

(Matthew 26:26-29; I Cor. 11: 20-30). This is because they are both symbolic of, and a memorial of, His death, burial, and resurrection.

Occasionally, the need to ordain a new minister would arise if a district lacked the full set of ministers. That consisted of a bishop, whose duty was to lead the flock and preach, two lay ministers, who also had the duty to preach, and one deacon. The deacon was responsible to police the flock. His obligations were to report any violations of the *Ordnung* or any questionable conduct to the Bishop. Consequently, he was often assigned the unpleasant task of investigating the situation and turning the offender over to the Bishop when necessary.

When an ordination was planned, it was held after the foot-washing ceremony. Each church member cast a secret vote. All the men with two or more votes were nominees for the lot; their names were then announced to the church, as everyone sat in fearful silence. Most men did not want their name to be among the nominees. On the other hand, there were a few who secretly desired the social honor of being the chosen one, according to their own inadvertent remarks following the event.

The appropriate number of hymnbooks were bound with a strip of cloth and placed on a small table. Already, the wives and relatives of the nominees were crying and hoping the burden would fall on the shoulders of someone else's husband. I dreaded the agonizing suspense as each nominee stepped up to the little table, took a hymnbook, and sat on the front bench, waiting for his book to be opened by the Bishop. The chosen one would be he in whose book a handwritten note containing a Bible verse was found tucked between the pages. With no further ceremony, he became a minister of the church.

Despite the fact that a man might rather die than carry the responsibility of preaching, he had no options. He was a minister for life if the book he chose contained that slip of paper. Volunteering, or being called by God into the ministry to preach or to be a missionary, was not an accepted stance to take. The philosophy was that God would direct His chosen one's hand to the book containing the note, based on Acts 1:26.

At the closing of the service, which by then resembled a funeral, many were weeping with sympathy for the newly ordained one. His new responsibility was considered to be a very serious position, a burden almost too holy to carry. In addition, there was often the dread of public speaking. His new position did not necessarily change his daily life, except he now needed to spend some time studying and memorizing scriptures prior to his turn to preach.

The men greeted the new minister with words of comfort and encouragement, while the ladies attempted to console his weeping wife. I stood helplessly by, wondering what words of comfort I could give in her time of distress.

The clock may have struck six by the time the people hurried home to do their evening chores.

The family of the newly ordained minister could expect a number of visitors at their home that evening. Many wanted to show their love and support and give encouragement to the family as they adjusted to the new burden.

My *dat* was in the lot numerous times but never happened to pick the book containing that life-changing slip of paper. Our family always experienced a great sense of relief when the Bishop handed the book back to *Dat,* indicating the note was not found inside, and proceeded on down the line.

The Greater Inheritance

Did You Know...

✓ Amish consider foot washing a part of keeping God's commandments.

The Greater Inheritance

Chapter Thirteen

Crossroads

*B*y late spring in our third year of marriage, my brother John married my friend Mattie, and moved to the neighboring community of Maywood. A month after they were married they came to visit us one weekend. They were again studying the Scriptures, and knew that our hunger for the truth was still alive. It had merely been pushed to the back of our minds for an extended period.

We spent that Saturday afternoon discussing Galatians 3 together, which proved to be a life-changing experience for us. We realized that the law was not a means by which to gain heaven, but rather a *schoolmaster* to show us that we cannot keep the law perfectly. We came to the startling realization that God's righteousness could not be obtained by flawlessly abiding by the church *Ordnung,* nor by adhering to a certain lifestyle.

I felt like a bird freed from its perpetual cage, yet dreadfully lost in a great big universe with no secure place to perch. We were desperately "fluttering our wings" in search of a safe place of refuge. As two lost, unrighteous sinners, we were utterly helpless to rescue our souls in the sight of a holy and righteous God. *As it is written, there is none righteous, no, not one* (Romans 3:10-12). Without a doubt, we knew

God had a solution to the lost condition of all mankind, although we could not yet fully comprehend it.

As John and Mattie continued to share the truths they had learned from the Bible, we found it hard to believe there was so much we had never heard. It was difficult to choose to believe those Scriptures that were in stark contrast with some of the teaching we had heard all our lives. We believed the Bible is the true Word of God. Nevertheless, we realized that both contradictory teachings could not be right. *Maybe we are misunderstanding something somewhere,* we speculated. We desired to make some sense of it all, and ...*searched the Scriptures daily, whether those things were so* (Acts 17:11).

Several weeks went by as John and I dealt with the ongoing turmoil in our souls. *How can we resist believing the Bible?* we wondered repeatedly. Yet, the overwhelming fear of claiming those truths that threatened the traditions taught by our parents and church leaders frustrated our progress. Causing family or church conflict was not our desire by any means. Consequently, for the sake of peace, Ervin and Elizabeth were the only people in our community with whom we could discuss Scriptures at that time. We kept in contact with John and Mattie and several like-minded friends from the Maywood community. That required the organization of a few secret meetings in order to avoid a public disturbance.

One evening, Ervin hired a driver to take him and Elizabeth, and John and me, to John and Mattie's house in Maywood. Some of our friends from that area, with mutual interests, joined us as well. That included my cousin Ida and her husband Glen, and John's brother Joe and his wife Rachel. We enjoyed a precious time of fellowship around God's Word.

94

We came home late that evening, nervous about the consequences, should others in our community learn where we had been. Our fears were compounded as we became aware that word was circulating in Maywood of some people "studying the Bible too much." Not much happened until the following week when John's parents and a brother and his wife went to visit the people in Maywood. They dutifully warned that part of our group about the danger of such Bible studies and the deceptive teaching of anything other than the interpretations and traditions our forefathers handed down to us.

At home, the atmosphere was getting a bit tense, to say the least, between our relatives and us. They heard that we were also studying the Bible, and they feared we were "playing with fire."

In September, John's sister Emma was married to Dannie at the family homestead. All of his brothers and sisters and their families came from other communities and out of state. It was a miserable day for a few of our group who had been involved in the Bible studies. But the grace of God would again prove to be sufficient.

That afternoon, after many of the guests had left, several of John's brothers and in-laws, and his *dat,* had a meeting with John's brother Joe from Maywood behind the barn. They warned him, in no uncertain terms, of the danger he was leading his family into if he continued to give heed to the *"fremda glawva"* (strange belief), as they described it. Evidently, it did not matter that the Bible says to correct "in love." They were exceedingly upset about the *"fremda glawva"* that threatened to destroy the family ties. They apparently assumed there is power in numbers as they each tried to convince Joe to stay off "the road to hell." They were sure to remind him that all of us needed to stay with the teachings of our forefathers, be obedient to our parents as the Bible says, and keep our promise to stay with the church. They did not want to hear anything from Joe's viewpoint, for fear of being deceived. They were certain that the Amish way of life was the only means by which one could please God and perhaps earn a home in heaven. We knew they were genuinely concerned for our souls, but it grieved our hearts to hear them reject what we believed to be Scriptural truths.

A few weeks later, a meeting was called at John's parents' house with some of the brothers and sisters, my parents, and some older men of the community, along with Ervin and Elizabeth and us. It mainly centered on our interest in the *"fremda glawva"*. Little consideration was given to our viewpoint. Their mission was to convince our group to repent from heading down a "dangerous path." They were sincerely concerned about keeping all their children within the Amish fold, although we had never mentioned any plans of leaving.

Naturally, we did not look forward to such stressful meetings, where emotions were high and misunderstandings ran deep. How we had to depend on God's grace to carry us through! The tension level was rapidly increasing day by day.

The following Monday, John's brother and family came to visit from southern Missouri. The brothers' and sisters' families in the area came together in their honor as usual. As could be expected, they were sure to turn the conversation to the *"fremda glawva"*. We tried to avoid arguments as much as possible. They had no intentions whatsoever of considering anything from our perspective. In their opinion, there was absolutely no possibility that we could be correct in our understanding of the Bible. The fact that it conflicted with some of the traditional Amish teachings was proof enough to them that we were seriously mistaken about the Bible truths we were claiming. It was a very unpleasant and disheartening evening for us. Again, we sought the Lord for strength and guidance.

Our generally very enjoyable family gatherings were sadly turning into dreaded events from everyone's standpoint. Despite the attitude of many of them, John's mother and younger sisters were generally kind and respectful to us through those difficult times, although we knew they were hurting and grieving inside. Our feelings were the same.

As the pressures of our situation increased, so did our need for encouragement from God's Word. About a week after that family gathering, we went to Maywood again for another Bible study. Again, we had to face the consequences. The following evening both John's parents and mine, along with several preachers, came to our house for a surprise visit. They were convinced by then that we were "going astray." We could not possibly be on the right path while disobeying our parents, they warned us. Their serious misunderstanding of us caused great sorrow and grief to their hearts, as well as ours. *What if they are right, and we are wrong?* crossed our minds once again. Oh, the agony of standing at the crossroads!

But then again, we encountered Scriptures that propelled us ever onward, such as Matthew10:37 and others, *He that loveth father or mother more than me is not worthy of me: and he that loveth son or daughter more than me is not worthy of me.*

It was soon apparent that the Lord would not allow us to linger miserably at the daunting crossroads. Certainly, we recognized the road to peace with the Amish church, and the road leading to peace with God. Sadly, they were undeniably two different roads. And there was no middle road for the indecisive. We were reminded of Joshua's words in Joshua 24:15, *Choose you this day whom ye will serve.* We realized we must choose the road to peace with God, despite the dictates of the Amish church.

Did You Know...

✓ Amish parents consider their childrearing a success if all of their children remain within the dominion of Amish churches.

Chapter Fourteen

Decisions

By mid-December in 1983, the part of our study group in Maywood was excommunicated because of a double offense. The first was refusing to adhere to the traditions and *Ordnung* taught by the church. The second offense was their refusal to deny the *"fremda glawva"* and spiritual freedom they had discovered. Those who were excommunicated were Bishop Yoder (Glen's father), Glen, Joe, John, and their wives.

John and I, along with Ervin and Elizabeth, still in the Bowling Green community, were now in serious violation of the shunning practices if we kept associating with them. Of course, we were not willing to deny everything we had learned thus far and break fellowship with them. As Daniel, who was forbidden to pray openly three times a day but continued to pray *as he did aforetime,*[4] we also were compelled to study the Scriptures as we did afore time, despite the cost.

---

[4] Daniel 6:10 *Now when Daniel knew that the writing was signed, he went into his house; and his windows being open in his chamber toward Jerusalem, he kneeled upon his knees three times a day, and prayed, and gave thanks before his God, as he did aforetime.*

Unquestionably, the dark storm cloud of excommunication was quickly rising over the horizon of our future. As a result, one peace-disturbing thought lingered in our hearts. It was that of receiving the Lord's free gift of salvation, only to lose it when the church excommunicated us. Thus, we determined to find out what the Bible, indeed, says about the security of the gift of salvation.

As John and I searched the Scriptures for an answer, it remained unclear to us until one morning in early January, one month after the excommunications in Maywood. As we studied John 10, it was as if verses 28 and 29 jumped right out at us. There we read that no one can pluck us out of God's hand once we are His sheep. "No man" includes even me! No man can corrupt or take away the complete and perfect salvation that only God can give us. *Who are kept by the power of God through faith unto salvation ready to be revealed in the last time* (I Peter 1:5). *For I know whom I have believed, and am persuaded that he is able to keep that which I have committed unto him against that day* (II Timothy 1:12).

We realized that the Bible says even the church ban cannot take away our salvation! The fact that God has said it is incorruptible, sealed,[5] and eternal tells us that it is none else but imperishable, ceaseless, and permanent. I Peter 1:23 tells us that we are *born again, not of corruptible seed, but of incorruptible, by the word of God, which liveth and abideth forever.* Jesus said, *Many will say to me in that day, Lord, Lord, have we not...in thy name done many wonderful works? And then will I profess unto them, I never knew you: depart from me, ye that work iniquity* (Matthew 7:22-23). Jesus obviously did not say they were once His but sin had cut them off. In spite of their

---

[5] Ephesians 1:13, *In whom ye also trusted, after that ye heard the word of truth, the gospel of your salvation: in whom also after that ye believed, ye were sealed with that holy Spirit of promise.*

good works He said, *I never knew you,* saying they were never His at any time—never. He is the great Shepherd, and He does not lose any of His sheep. *And this is the Father's will which hath sent me, that of all which he hath given me I should lose nothing, but should raise it up again at the last day* (John 6:39).

We realized that salvation is not something that God gives us one day and takes away the next, depending on our righteous conduct or lack thereof. If such were the case, salvation would be dependent on us rather than on God. Granted, unrighteous conduct will quench, or silence, the Holy Spirit and break our fellowship with God; but it will not cause Him to reject us, nor break His promise of salvation to us. *I will never leave thee, nor forsake thee* (Hebrews 13:5). Repentance will restore that fellowship and communication with God through the Spirit. We were incredibly relieved that our eternal destiny is not dependent on our holding on to God, but that God is the one firmly holding on to us, having sealed us with the earnest of the Spirit.[6] He gives His children the Holy Spirit as the earnest of His promise. An earnest payment cannot be taken back in the financial or in the spiritual realm. Therefore, the Holy Spirit is ours forever upon receiving salvation by faith. He cannot leave us because of I John 5:7 and other scriptures; *the Father, the Word* (Son), *and the Holy Ghost…these three are one.* They are inseparable.

I believe that was the day I fully realized Christ has done it all, and the only right choice was to accept that and receive Him as my Savior. Christ said, *It is finished.*[7] I then repented of the sin of rejecting Him and trusting in any of my own efforts to gain heaven. I bowed my knees before a Holy God, in acceptance of His payment for my salvation.

---

[6] II Corinthians 1:22, *Who hath also sealed us, and given the earnest of the Spirit in our hearts.*

[7] John 19:30, *…It is finished: and he bowed his head, and gave up the ghost.*

Acts 4:12 says, *Neither is there salvation in any other: for there is none other name under heaven given among men, whereby we must be saved.* Romans 4:25 says, *Who was delivered for our offences, and was raised again for our justification.* Isaiah 53:5 tells us *But he was wounded for our transgressions, he was bruised for our iniquities: the chastisement of our peace was upon him; and with his stripes we are healed.* John also accepted the Lord as his Savior about that time.

We did not claim a license to do as we pleased when we claimed salvation, as many Amish people suppose. But we received a new desire to please Him as our Lord, rather than pleasing man and our own flesh. Hebrews 11:6 says, *But without faith it is impossible to please Him.* As His child we now had a greater responsibility to obey the truths, which the Holy Spirit had shown us. To please Him is to be filled and controlled by His Spirit. Only then could we produce the works of the Christian: *love, joy, peace*...(Galatians 5:22).

Jesus rescued us when He paid a debt He did not owe, because we owed a debt we could not pay. Salvation is a gift to us.[8] What great love He has for unworthy sinners![9] He deserves to be Lord of my life. *Ye are bought with a price; be not ye the servants of men* (I Corinthians 7:23).

Romans 10:13 says, *For whosoever shall call upon the name of the Lord shall be saved.* Jesus also told Nicodemus in John 3:3, *Except a man be born again, he cannot see the kingdom of God.* According to these Scriptures, and many others, we are not born-again collectively, or as a group. We understood it

---

[8] Ephesians 2:8-9, *For by grace are ye saved through faith; and that not of yourselves: it is the gift of God: not of works, lest any man should boast.*

[9] John 3:16; I John 4:10, Romans 5:8, But *God commendeth His love toward us, in that, while we were yet sinners, Christ died for us.*

to mean that each individual soul must accept Him personally.

As the next few days went by in a blur, inevitable changes were beginning to become a reality. We realized that many of those changes would undoubtedly be emotionally difficult for everyone involved. Only our Lord knew when or how soon we would have to face those difficulties. Nevertheless, we had confidence that He would meet us there. He is *my strength, and my redeemer* (Psalms 19:14).

Although we had many days of peace and strength in our Lord concerning the decisions we had to make along the way, we also had our days of wrong focus and discouragement. One of those low days sneaked up on me one morning as I was alone in the kitchen. I was nearly overwhelmed when I tried to comprehend how the anticipated changes would soon utterly turn our world upside down. Instead of washing the dishes right after breakfast, I stacked them and sat down on the mini-trampoline next to the pantry door. I laid back on it, staring at the ceiling, while hundreds of thoughts raced wildly through my mind. Those thoughts soon gave way to tears as I considered all the hearts and family ties that would surely be broken because of our decision to do that which we sincerely believed to be our Lord's leading. How our hearts ached, yet we desired to follow that leading, no matter the cost.

Later that morning, John and I discussed some of the predictable consequences, while trying to prepare ourselves mentally for the inevitable. Certainly, we would be excommunicated from the church, which did not disturb us much anymore. However, we would be severely shunned as well. We could expect rude and spiteful treatment from those we cared about the most, and from others who had claimed to be our friends. We would definitely be separated from our families. Especially our daughter Rosa, almost three years old, would miss *Grosmommy*. She always looked forward to having Rosa come across the yard to see her every day. Her heart would be broken in a thousand pieces. We would have to move out of our little house that we appreciated so much. We would never have the opportunity, as was expected, to live in the big house where John grew up. We had been expected to take over the family farm, since John was the youngest son, and live on the home place. We would not be invited to our sisters' weddings. We would enjoy no more jolly family get-togethers with fresh strawberries and seven or eight freezers of homemade ice cream lined up on the sidewalk. Those were times when dozens of cousins together created fond, lasting memories. We would be cut off from all earthly inheritance, which would be no small sum.

The list went on and on until our Lord reminded us that He is our Rock and our Strength. Psalms 61:2, *...when my heart is overwhelmed: lead me to the rock that is higher than I.* He was the only One whom we could trust to sustain us through the impending storm. He would pick up and mend the broken pieces left in its devastating path. We praise our Lord that He did not allow us to see in advance all the stormy valleys we would have to cross to reach the mountaintop!

After much prayer, Scripture studying and putting things back in the right perspective, we realized our only right option was to continue going forward. Doing otherwise would have meant denying the great Truth we had come to love and hunger for so much. *But whosoever shall deny me before men, him will I also deny before my Father which is in heaven* (Matthew 10:33).

The Scriptures also reminded us that temporal and earthly things could not be compared to the gift of eternal life and having the assurance thereof. The joy of knowing Christ Himself is better than all else. Philippians 3:8...*For whom I have suffered the loss of all things, and do count them but dung, that I may win Christ.*

Shortly after that decisive day, at almost eleven o'clock on a Saturday night, we were surprised by a peculiar tapping on our living room window. Alarmed, we wondered who could be calling on us at that time of the night. Was someone playing a prank on us? We were soon to discover that it was none else but Glen and my brother John from Maywood. Providentially, we were not yet in bed.

One of them had their own vehicle by then and had it parked close to our "English" neighbors' house. They had walked the rest of the way so they would not be suspected by anyone. We quickly let them in and had a Bible study until about two o'clock in the morning. Each time we met for a study, we were refreshed and encouraged, and our faith always increased!

The next day's church service was the last time we planned to attend; however, no one in church was aware of that yet. The preachers knew of our Bible studies, and had their quivers crammed with verbal daggers intended to pierce our hearts. Sadly, they chose to use our situation as subject material, rather than preach the Bible only. We did not wish to be their target any longer. Of course, we did not tell our parents, or anyone else who opposed us, that we did not plan to attend their church services again. We could only imagine their reaction, had we told them, and we were not gluttons for punishment!

The following week, John's brothers and in-laws who lived in the area came over to cut several months' supply of firewood. They would do this for each of them in turn until they all had their winter's supply of firewood.

John was nervous all day, knowing they would very likely tackle him about the Bible study issue.

They worked until dark that evening. Some left for home then, while several stayed and followed John into our back porch to give him a piece of their mind. Their mission appeared to be to force him to change his mind. He must have felt as if he were in a "den of lions," being chewed up verbally.

Meanwhile, I was helplessly pacing the floor in the living room, praying and wishing they would leave. It nearly put my stomach in knots, wondering if they were going to barge in at any moment and lecture me too.

At last, John could tolerate it no longer. He slipped through the kitchen door and quickly locked it behind him. I was so proud of him for his bravery! The attackers had no choice but to go on home. It must have been extremely frustrating for them to see their "little brother" refuse to comply with their demands. That was not the brother they had known for over twenty years!

Naturally, sleep did not come very easily for us that night. We needed an enormous portion of God's grace to face the morrow.

The next evening, John went to use an English neighbor's phone to call Glen in Maywood, who now had his own phone. It was time for a breath of fresh air. As always, we were greatly encouraged. We also corresponded regularly by letters with Glen and Ida, and John and Mattie.

The following day, my brother Jerry and his wife Fannie, and my Uncle Harvey and his wife Rosa, from

The Greater Inheritance

Michigan, and Aunt Mattie from Indiana came to our house for lunch. What a surprise! It was good to see them, but we also knew what their mission was. They were kind and respectful while warning us of the worldly dangers out there. We could not help but appreciate their approach, even though we did not agree on everything.

Uncle Harvey was concerned about us getting involved in worldly matters, such as medical and life insurance. Fannie was quite positive that Jesus would use a buggy too, as they do, for transportation if He were here in today's world. She did not believe He would approve at all of having a motorized vehicle. We knew that according to the Bible, Jesus utilized the most modern form of transportation available at that time, which was either a donkey, or boat, or whatever was available. There is not even a hint that it was ever an issue to Him. Nevertheless, we summoned a measure of self-control and refrained from asking them by what form of transportation they came to admonish us. Not being behind the steering wheel makes all the difference, in the Amish man's opinion.

That weekend went by smoothly, since it was not our district's Sunday to have church. Ervin and Elizabeth lived in the other district, and it was the first Sunday they stopped attending church there.

Did You Know...

✓ In most Amish churches, the members' outward appearances, obedience to the *Ordnung* and traditions, and the keeping of commandments are referred to as Christian works, or the fruit of the Spirit. That is perceived as evidence that one may be going to heaven, or is at least on the right path.

✓ In many communities, all family members who leave the Amish circles are denied any family inheritance. However, there may be a few in the less conservative churches who do not take it to that extent.

✓ Amish people do not carry medical or any other kind of insurance. Some, however, do participate in a Brotherhood program, helping one another with medical bills. Their church will also help when the need arises.

Chapter Fifteen

Knock, Knock

*T*he following Wednesday evening we had another Bible study. That time we met at Ervin and Elizabeth's house, which was almost seven miles from us. It turned out to be the most memorable one of all!

A former Amish friend from Maywood, along with Glen, Joe, and John and Mattie, came to take us to the meeting. Being after dark, they parked up the road a ways so as not to arouse suspicion by entering our driveway. John jumped out and came in the back way, running across the field and climbing over fences to get to our house. That enabled him to enter from the back of the house, out of sight from the neighbors.

Since we knew they were coming, we had our two little ones bundled up and prepared to leave quickly.

Trudging through several inches of snow, we followed him back across the fields, alongside the woods, and over the fences to the waiting van. We could almost imagine someone lurking in the dark behind the trees, ready to leap out, capture us, and turn us over to the church authorities. But the spine-chilling trek was not enough to keep us from the Bible study. We were eagerly anticipating another enjoyable evening around God's Word and were greatly relieved when we were safely inside the van at last!

Ervin and Elizabeth lived just across the yard from my parents' house, and we did not want to cause a disturbance by driving in their lane. It was close to midnight, and we expected my parents and sisters to be in bed. However, as an extra precaution, we parked up the road about a quarter mile from Ervin and Elizabeth's house, supposing the van to be out of view from my parent's house. Again, we crossed the fields, encountering two or three fences in our path. We had sufficient help to boost the two little ones over the fence. The rest of us helped each other through the tricky maneuvering of climbing the wobbly wire ladders without ripping too many ugly gashes in our clothes, or skin, for that matter. We could not prevent leaving telltale trails in the snow, which would be a dead giveaway the next morning. What an adventure! We did not mind the snow or obstacles at all; we were going to a Bible study!

Once safely inside their living room, we kept the oil lamp turned as low as possible to avoid any suspicion, if by any chance *Dat* should wake up and look out the window. How we longed to prevent heartaches, yet grow in the Lord. Secret meetings appeared to be our only solution thus far.

We were soon in deep discussion about the things Jesus taught His disciples. I well remember Glen teaching us about Peter's faith in walking on the water.[10] He reminded us to keep our eyes upon the Lord. Peter began sinking when he started looking at the storm waves around him. We

---

[10] Matthew 14:29, …And when Peter was come down out of the ship, he walked on the water, to go to Jesus.

likewise would become discouraged, and our faith would weaken, if we took our eyes off the Lord and focused on the storms of life, which were certainly raging around us. It was a great encouragement to us, and we were hungrily devouring every word.

Then abruptly, there was a firm "knock, knock, knock" on the front door!

The room became deathly quiet. Our hearts dropped to the bottom of our beings. *Oh, no, not tonight! This cannot be happening,* we groaned inwardly. Time seemed to stand still. It appeared all of us were frozen to our chairs, and no one wished to be the one to answer the door. We did not need to. All too soon, the door opened slowly, and there stood my parents in the doorway, utterly shocked and speechless. The feelings were mutual. What was there to say? We had been discovered disregarding the many warnings given us. There was no doubt; we were in an intense predicament with inevitably severe consequences.

As I recall, *Mem* was the first to respond, with an expression of utter dismay. She asked, *"Chon, vo sin dei gallus?"* (John, where are your suspenders?) He simply answered, *"Da hame"* (At home).

To abandon the suspenders was a sure indication that he was forsaking the old traditions and the church *Ordnung*. Apparently it was just *unbegreiflich* (unimaginable) that one of their own sons would commit such a dreadful deed. They were obviously shocked and deeply disappointed. *Dat* did not verbally express an opinion throughout the entire short ordeal, although the look on his face was nothing short of sheer horror.

One by one, we filed past *Dat* and *Mem* and out the door without comment. We assumed no number of justifiable explanations could have redeemed us. When I reached the door, *Mem* offered us a bed at their house, presumably so we would not need to ride home with a shunned driver. The only response that came to my dazed mind was to remind her, with all due respect, that we had a bed at home.

Undoubtedly, my parents wanted to rescue us from what they perceived to be the devil's worst trap. They were certain those forbidden Bible studies were leading us astray from the trusted traditions of our forefathers.

Our hearts were pained to see them so bitterly disappointed and hurting. How we longed to share with them what the Holy Spirit had revealed to us through the Scriptures, rather than see them grieve over our choice of letting the Bible be our guide. Our hearts ached to show them that being born again is undeniably through Christ alone,[11] and not through rules and traditions. Galatians 3:11, Romans 1:17, and Habakkuk 2:4 say, ...*the just shall live by faith.* Christianity is God reaching down to rescue man, while religion is man trying to reach up to God. Such an attempt on man's part is futile.

Our driver brought the van up to Ervin's house, and we were on our way home shortly. Once at home, he drove right up to our house. *What do we have to lose?* we reasoned. The episode would undoubtedly be community news the next day anyway.

In the wee hours of the morning, we dropped into bed with heavy hearts and mixed feelings, only to lie there struggling with the many questions that robbed us of some

---

[11] Gal.2:16; Titus 3:5, Not by works of righteousness which we have done, but according to his mercy he saved us, by the washing of regeneration, and renewing of the Holy Ghost.

much-needed sleep. *What does the Lord want us to do next?* we wondered.

How we yearned to practice the Scriptures according to our understanding, without destroying family peace and unity! We were forced to face the fact that a life controlled primarily by tradition and *Ordnung* cannot coexist with a life guided entirely by the Bible, as indicated in the book of Mark.[12] We knew God's Word, and not the *Ordnung*, must be supreme in our lives. And He, not the Amish church, would guide us through every situation. With such comforting thoughts, we drifted off to a peaceful sleep.

Did You Know...

✓ In most communities, church members are forbidden to ride with an excommunicated driver. To do so usually results in a mandatory confession of sin before the congregation.

---

[12] Mark 7:13, *Making the word of God of none effect through your tradition...*

View from back of our house

View from our front yard looking toward the big house

Our former driving horse

Chapter Sixteen

Oppositions

*T*wo days later, my parents brought my Uncle Menno and his wife, who were from Michigan, for a visit. They deemed it their duty to come to Missouri to warn and advise us to reconsider our choices. We appreciated their respectful attitude and willingness to listen to our viewpoint, although they could not agree with us.

Then it was Sunday again. We were quite nervous, to say the least. Staying at home when our church was having a service was sure to bring some uninvited and concerned visitors to our door.

As expected, in the afternoon, John's parents, along with two of his brothers and their wives, came over to "set us straight." Naturally, they could not accept the fact that we would not want to go to their church anymore. The ladies wept, but mostly kept silent, while their husbands told us what a terrible eternity we would face if we did not repent.

They also warned us, as they had many times before, of the Scriptures instructing us to obey our parents. The church holds strongly to their favorite teachings such as

Ephesians 6:1 and 2.[13] They evidently perceive the phrase *in the Lord* to mean Amish, and demand unconditional loyalty to the parents. However, the Bible says, *We ought to obey God rather than men (*Acts 5:29). As we understand the Scriptures, obeying God sometimes requires us to deny our parents' wishes. However, we ought to always endeavor to honor them as our parents. We believe God gives young people, who marry and establish an independent home, the responsibility to make their own choices, and obey God above all else.

Since we knew that their mission was not to listen to us that Sunday afternoon, we chose not to respond much in order to avoid an argument. Our silence seemed to frustrate them. After admonishing us for a while, one of them commented about not being able to accomplish much without our response, and decided they might as well leave. As they went out the door, one brother remarked, "We might as well shake the dust off our feet and leave."[14] With all due respect, we were relieved when the unpleasant visit was over. The strain on family relationships was becoming more distressing every day.

The following Tuesday was butchering day for John's parents and us. Several of the family came over to help process a beef and several hogs, which was to be our supply of meat for the year. We were allowed to work with them since we were not excommunicated yet, but the atmosphere was rather tense. It was an all-day process,

---

[13] Ephesians 6:1-2, *Children, obey your parents in the Lord: for this is right. Honour thy father and mother; which is the first commandment with promise.*

[14] Matthew 10:14, *And whosoever shall not receive you, nor hear your words, when ye depart out of that house or city, shake off the dust of your feet.*

The Greater Inheritance

beginning early in the morning with scalding the hogs in a tank of hot water after they were slain. The beef had been skinned the previous day, and then cut up that day, along with the pork. Most of the beef, except the stew meat, was ground up and canned. The pork hams and bacon were kept back to cure later, while the rest of it was made into stuffed sausage and liverwurst.

That day, another one of John's brothers and his wife arrived from southern Missouri. Certainly, their goal was also to warn us against the *"fremda glawva"*. The next evening we had a family gathering at John's parents' house in their honor. We groaned deep within our souls, knowing we were the chief reason for the get-together, and what we could expect to endure before the evening was over. We longed to escape somewhere, just anywhere but there.

Our longing for an escape intensified the next day when another brother and his wife from southern Missouri came for the second time. That meant two consecutive family gatherings in one week! *How many times must we listen to their doom saying?* we wondered wearily. But once again, our Lord was faithful, giving us strength to survive both ordeals.

After a week filled with tense butchering days and two stressful family gatherings, we knew we were in great need of some encouragement again.

A few days later on Sunday, we went with our "English" neighbors to Maywood to attend the evening church service at a Baptist church for the first time. Ervin and Elizabeth were there as well. What a wonderful and refreshing message we heard that evening!

Joe, Glen, John, and their families had attended the Baptist church several times already before we did. They had received a flier in the mail, inviting them to an ordination service at the Baptist church. Out of curiosity,

Glen and Joe decided to take their families and attend the event. To their great amazement, they discovered the church believed the same doctrine they had been learning from the Bible!

Later, we visited other churches in that area as well, but could not agree entirely with any other than the Baptist church. Pastor Stowe, who was there at that time, was exceedingly patient with us as we adjusted to the drastically unfamiliar culture. That was only the beginning of the many years we would attend that church.

The services were carried out in an entirely different fashion than they were at the Amish church from which we came. We realized it would be difficult to adjust to such a strange environment. Families sat together during the service, which lasted only about an hour. Musical instruments accompanied the singing, as the Bible speaks of in the book of Psalms.[15] No lunch was served after the service, and we went home after an enjoyable visit with new friends. We knew the different method of conducting the service was not unscriptural, but it was unlike anything we had ever experienced. That was only one aspect of the culture shock we would experience. Yet, we knew we would be back soon to receive more nourishment for the soul.

It came as no surprise that we had visitors again the next evening. After we had finished dinner, the door opened and several uninvited Amish preachers walked into

---

[15] Psalms 33:2, *Praise the LORD with harp: sing unto him with the psaltery and an instrument of ten strings.*

Psalms 144:9, *I will sing a new song unto thee, O God: upon a psaltery and an instrument of ten strings will I sing praises unto thee.*

our living room. They proceeded to warn us that unless we repented and came back to their church, we would have to be excommunicated. We listened respectfully to what they had to say, but responded minimally, knowing without a doubt what our decision would be.

It was not a joyful thought to be excommunicated, since it meant stringent separation from family and friends. On the other hand, our hope was that excommunication might enable us to live a more peaceful personal life as a family again, without daily disturbances and attempts to discourage. However, we soon learned that was wishful thinking at best.

The following Friday afternoon we had a vanload of relatives come from another community to warn us about the "dangerous path" we were taking. They apparently felt certain it would lead us straight to the pits of hell. Their accusations were that we were forsaking the Amish traditions and church *Ordnung,* forfeiting all probability of earning a home in heaven.

They evidently did not consider Mark 7:7-8, where Jesus warned the Pharisees about *teaching for doctrines the commandments of men,* making the words of men equal to the Word of God. He went on to say, *For laying aside the commandment of God, ye hold the tradition of men.* Jesus knew the Pharisees were extremely precise in keeping their rules and traditions, supposing it would make them righteous.

No one worked more diligently in trying to obtain perfect righteousness by their deeds than the scribes and Pharisees. Yet, Jesus called them hypocrites. He warns in Matthew 5:20, *For I say unto you, That except your righteousness shall exceed the righteousness of the scribes and Pharisees, ye shall in no case enter into the kingdom of heaven.*

But to exceed the righteousness of the scribes and Pharisees, one would have to be virtually perfect. We would all admit that no one is perfect. Yet, that is exactly what Jesus commands at the end of that chapter: *Be ye therefore perfect, even as your Father which is in heaven is perfect* (Matthew 5:48).

We must then conclude that He is not speaking of human perfection, but of divine perfection, without which one cannot enter the Kingdom of God. Only the Savior can clothe us with that cloak of perfect righteousness when we put our trust in Him, and none else, for eternal life. Any attempts to achieve salvation by adding our own righteousness would be a corrupt salvation; the two cannot be intermingled. However, these truths were utterly rejected and ignored by the load of visitors that day.

We went to Ervin and Elizabeth's house that evening and had an enjoyable and refreshing time. We were just trying to keep our heads above the roaring waves of the stormy sea at that time!

The next day, Saturday, another one of John's brothers from southern Missouri came to see us. By then, our house was apparently a community center, attracting people from all directions. In the Amish culture, rejecting one's own people as visitors was inconceivable, causing us to believe our only option was to be hospitable to anyone who came to see us.

The next morning, we enjoyed the Baptist church again. The day of peaceful fellowship went by incredibly fast. We came on home after the evening service.

Once again, the next evening it was time for another family get-together, since John's brother was still there. By then, our challengers were beginning to realize their efforts to keep us under their regime were rather futile, and the admonitions were becoming a bit less severe. However, the atmosphere was still dreadfully tense. By the grace of God, we endured it without too much difficulty.

We also had a few other visitors in the following weeks who were not relatives but felt compelled to come and give us their opinion regarding the step we were taking.

One question we were asked frequently was, "How can you break the promise you made to the church on your knees in baptism?" That is the ultimate sin in their opinion.

The first part of that promise is: *Do you renounce the world, the devil with all his subtle ways, as well as your own flesh and blood, and desire to serve Jesus Christ alone, who died on the cross for you?* Obviously, their interpretation of *the world* was everything that is not in agreement with the Amish lifestyle. But we could not truly keep this segment of the promise until we let go of the *Ordnung* and all human attempts to earn salvation. Only then could we allow Him to be Lord and Savior of our life, and "serve Jesus Christ alone."

Violating the second part of that promise is inconceivable in their minds. It asks, *Do you also promise before God and His church that you will support these teachings and regulations [church Ordnung] with the Lord's help, faithfully attend the services of the church and help to counsel and work in it, and not forsake it, whether it leads you to life or to death?*

Our answer is found in Acts 17:30, *And the times of this ignorance God winked at; but now commandeth all men every where to repent*—be saved. We do not believe God holds us to a promise that, according to His Word, should never have been made. We were ignorant of the fact that fulfilling that promise would not result in salvation, but is actually contrary to God's Word. Christ commands *all men* to repent from trusting in all else, and trust Him alone for salvation. We realized such a promise or vow required by men, when

Scripture does not require it, is not binding, and is nothing short of erroneous teaching.

Never in the Bible was anyone asked to make a vow or promise before being baptized. Even our ancestors, whom the Amish leaders greatly admire, deemed it right to break their vows to their mother church when they judged those vows to be unscriptural. They too were willing to endure the afflictions placed upon them by the church.

We are thankful that God forgave us of that promise when He put all our sins under the blood when we received Him as our Lord and Savior.

We could no longer support a church that required its members to adhere to the *Ordnung* and traditions in an effort to obtain righteousness. The main function of that baptismal promise, though, is apparently to maintain control of the church members. The leaders are permitted to use almost any method to keep them within the set boundaries. That includes the claim of power to condemn one to hell, and the claim that abandoning their teachings and *Ordnung* is to abandon God.

Kindly expressing a sincere concern *in love* happened occasionally, but most seemed to prefer the persuasion by intimidation method. Regardless of the circumstances, James 1:20 will always stand true, *For the wrath of man worketh not the righteousness of God.* One church member who came to reprimand us obviously did not recognize this Scripture. We stood speechless as he raised his voice in our faces, venting his judgment of us to his own satisfaction. With hardly a comment, we watched him leave, a bit winded and red-faced. We did not feel such an undignified outburst deserved a response. If his mission was to draw us back to his religion, he had definitely failed. He successfully inspired us to continue marching forward in our decision to follow the truth of the Bible. We realized that the poor, blinded soul desperately needed the Lord.

As we continued to attend the Baptist church, the people in our community began to realize our intentions to keep going forward. The number of visitors slowly dwindled.

Did You Know...

✓ Skipping church services for any reason other than sickness or travel is considered a major offense and is punishable by excommunication if the member does not repent and attend church again.

Chapter Seventeen

Shunned

On the first Sunday in March of 1984, we were excommunicated from the Amish church. Of course, we were not there to hear the verdict, but someone made sure to inform us. Although we knew we would no longer be tolerated in the church as a member, we had a sense of relief, and a peace that only our Lord could give us.

Later, we were told one of the men in the congregation wept aloud when he heard the ban being pronounced on us. We were reminded of Jesus' words in Luke 23:28, when He said *"...weep not for me, but weep for yourselves, and for your children." If only they could see the truth,* we lamented.

The next day we went to Maywood to prepare a small rental house for us and Ervin and Elizabeth, as we were all moving to Maywood. We would share the house for a few weeks.

We were able to pack and get ready to make the move without too many interruptions by then. Of course, we could not expect any help from anyone in the community, since we were excommunicated and they did not want to give the impression of endorsing our move.

That week we also made another visit to our wonderful "English" neighbors, who were a great encouragement to us through the entire experience and even provided transportation to Maywood for us on numerous occasions.

We moved out of the Bowling Green community in mid-March. It was a day we had eagerly anticipated, yet dreaded to face because of the potentially difficult departure. We realized that only by the grace of God would we survive the day victoriously.

Rosa had spent the night with her aunts over in the other house. She was excited about that, but I am sure her aunts and *grosdawdy* and *grosmommy* were very brokenhearted. Our hearts ached with empathy. At such times when the burdens seemed too heavy to bear, Scriptures such as Romans 8:18 were a blessed encouragement to us: *For I reckon that the sufferings of this present time are not worthy to be compared with the glory which shall be revealed in us.*

We had hired a driver from town, whom we knew quite well, to bring his pickup truck and stock trailer to move our belongings. We did not have much but were thankful for the driver's help in loading our few household possessions. None of our relatives were allowed to, nor desired to, aid us in our decision to leave the Amish culture and religion.

Several of John's siblings and families had gathered in the other house with John's parents to comfort each other during that time. With everything loaded before noon, we had the dreaded task of going over to the other house to bid them good-bye.

When we walked into the living room, we were a bit stunned at the scene, which somewhat resembled a funeral. One sister was wailing aloud, while others were sobbing uncontrollably. What were we to do or say? Our sincere attempts to comfort them only resulted in receiving a cold shoulder. What an utterly helpless feeling! Our hearts throbbed with pain as we observed the inconsolable group mourning over our decision to follow God's leading. Obviously, they were certain it was the devil leading us, rather than the Lord.

One brother asked us why we did not break down and weep likewise. John commented that we believed we were making the right decision, although we regretted causing them inevitable heartaches. They remained unconvinced of the Lord's involvement in the situation.

We were thankful that both three-year-old Rosa and one-year-old Omar were too young to grasp the finality and traumatic ending of that era of our lives.

Our almighty God alone deserves all the praise and glory for the emotional and physical strength we experienced to walk out of that living room and out of the only way of life we had ever known.

A brother-in-law followed us outside to the waiting truck. He earnestly warned us again that by going out into the "world," we not only endangered our very lives, but also our marriage would become vulnerable to Satan's attacks. As we closed the truck door, his last words to us were that he was almost certain that in two years John and I would not be together anymore,[16] if we stayed out in the "world." Evidently, he assumed that leaving the security of the

---

[16] In 2005, John and I joyfully celebrated twenty-five blessed years together! "To God be the glory, great things He hath done," in His omniscience, bringing us together. We are eagerly anticipating the next twenty-five years together!

Amish *Ordnung* and lifestyle would automatically result in a wicked lifestyle of divorce, ungodly children, and many other sinful practices.

With that difficult segment of our moving day behind us, we went over to Ervin and Elizabeth's house where we filled the rest of the trailer with their belongings. My parents and sisters from across the yard did not help them load either.

Although we had no intent of disrespect, we did not go over to my parents' house to bid them good-bye before we left. We simply did not think we could bear to confront another round of emotionally painful good-byes. By mid-afternoon, Ervin and Elizabeth, with their two small children, also turned their backs to the only life and culture they had ever known.

We were soon on our way to a new life of freedom in Christ, a new home, in a new environment, in a new culture! How could a soul contain such joy and sorrow simultaneously? Joy in freedom to serve our Lord, yet sorrow in leaving behind a trail of broken hearts. They are in our prayers daily.

We had an abundance of help unloading our belongings when we arrived at our temporary home in Maywood. By evening, we had the furniture and other basic items in decent order. We were physically and emotionally drained, and certainly ready to retire at bedtime. Yet we went to bed knowing God had been good to us, and we were blessed beyond measure.

Chapter Eighteen

Adapting

*J*ohn and I, along with some others of our group, were baptized by immersion about a week after we moved. That was an extremely offensive issue to our Amish relatives. They did not agree with the biblical mode of baptism by immersion.[17] It seemed rather obvious to us since Jesus himself was baptized in the river, and John was baptizing where there was *much water*.[18] Philip and the eunuch *went down both into the water...and he baptized him* (Acts 8:38). That would not have been necessary had a bucket of water been sufficient.

The original meaning of the word *baptize* is to dip, to immerse, to plunge under completely. We also learned that this mode of baptism pictures Christ's death, burial, and resurrection. Without immersion, it is rather difficult to

---

[17] Matthew 3:16, *And Jesus, when he was baptized, went up straightway out of the water: and, lo, the heavens were opened unto him, and he saw the Spirit of God descending like a dove, and lighting upon him.*

[18] John 3:23, *And John also was baptizing in Aenon near to Salim, because there was much water there: and they came, and were baptized.*

picture being buried with Christ and raised to walk in newness of life with Him.

Baptism was a step of our obedience to the Lord[19] because our sins had been remitted. It was not a means by which to obtain salvation, but a testimony of having received salvation.[20] In the Bible, we read of many souls who were saved without the opportunity of baptism, or without the mention of baptism, since that was not a part of salvation.

Before long, we were buying clothes instead of making everything we wore. At first, it was difficult for us to match the right colors and pieces. It was quite embarrassing to learn, after we came home from church one Sunday, that one of the men in our group had been wearing a ladies' shirt to church! Another embarrassing incident involved mine and Elizabeth's little one-year-old boys. They still wore dresses at first, according to the Amish dress code, giving the nursery workers an exceedingly shocking revelation, never to be forgotten!

Through God's Word, we understood that God is not concerned with the color, texture, style, or the measurement of our clothing, as long as it modestly covers

---

[19] Acts 2:38, *Then Peter said unto them, Repent, and be baptized every one of you in the name of Jesus Christ for the remission of sins, and ye shall receive the gift of the Holy Ghost.*

[20] Acts 2:41, Then they that gladly received his word were baptized: and the same day there were added unto them about three thousand souls.

the body. We took modesty to mean dressing in a manner that is not suggestive or would not provoke lustful thoughts in the mind of the opposite gender. As Christian women, we did not wish to make their battle with the sin nature more difficult. Rom. 14:13 says, *but judge this rather, that no man put a stumbling block or an occasion to fall in his brother's way*. Our Christian testimony was at stake as well.

Therefore, we understood that we must appropriately cover our nakedness, as is becoming of a Christian. According to Scripture, a godly woman will clothe herself and her daughters *in modest apparel with shamefacedness and sobriety*. I Timothy 2:9 says, *In like manner also, that women adorn themselves in modest apparel, with shamefacedness and sobriety*.

We still did not feel comfortable without scarves to cover our heads. We continued to wear them for a few months, until we better understood the concept of I Corinthians 11:1-16. Through our pastor's preaching, and through studying the Scriptures, we learned what Paul was teaching concerning the man and the woman's head being covered or uncovered. Eventually, in verse 15 he clearly states that the covering of the woman's head is her hair. As we understood it, we did not need an additional covering.

In time, we established a daily routine of life again. The men started working odd jobs wherever they were available, and after a while, they each found a more permanent job. Entering the secular work world had its own challenges.

We were now neighbors to Joe, Glen, and John's families. Naturally, we spent much time together, helping each other adjust to our new surroundings and adapt to the new culture.

In April, John and Mattie welcomed their firstborn son Marvin into their family. When Marvin was a month old, they wanted to present him to his *grosdawdy* and *grosmommy,* and decided to go back to Bowling Green for a visit.

Ervin's family and we accompanied them. It was our first visit since we had moved, and not a very pleasant one. Although they did allow us inside the house, we were told not to bring our vehicle onto their property again.

Sadly, not one of the six sisters or *grosmommy* held the new baby, but basically ignored him. While not surprised by their lack of hospitality, we all were deeply disappointed at their rejection of their new grandbaby. That was only the first of several unpleasant visits with them. Prayer was our only answer to the difficult situation.

My parents then moved to Michigan that same year. We were happy to see them move to a community that allowed more freedoms that are biblical.

Our first year in Maywood was filled with countless strange and unparalleled experiences. In June, John experienced the adventure of learning to drive and getting his driver's license. In July, we bought our first vehicle, a silver, '76 Ford LTD station wagon, for seven hundred dollars. I eventually had the courage to get my license in the fall. That was an experience in itself!

I am sure God protected us from many accidents in those first few months, although a few farm implements, trees, posts, and such that seemed to mysteriously appear in our path had some dangerously narrow escapes. The car's brake pedal and accelerator were much more sensitive than a horse's reins, and at times even seemed to switch their positions unexpectedly. I also learned that pulling on the steering wheel did not produce the same results as pulling on the horse's reins, when I nearly ran over Joe's plow sitting beside their driveway. Whew! I was glad we did not have to repair or replace that plow, not to mention our old Ford station wagon.

What an incredible sense of freedom, without condemnation! No more would we need to disturb a neighbor to go distances too far for a horse to travel. Also, there was no more need for unconvincing attempts to rationalize to the driver our eagerness to occupy the passenger side, while absolutely refusing to take control of the wheel. That objection was presumably based on a misconception of using but not abusing the world.[21]

Freezing our fresh garden produce, as an alternative to canning, was a much healthier and more convenient option that we now had. We were repeatedly amazed at the fresh taste of frozen fruits and vegetables. We were denied that privilege all those years when we were required to can everything.

Another major event in that first year took place in June when we received the sad news that John's *mem*, age sixty-five, had passed away. The family lost a sweet and precious "jewel" when her petite body succumbed to her battle with a heart disease for many years.

We did not look forward to going to the visitation and the funeral. Meeting many of the relatives for the first time since we had moved was sure to be a distressing day. However, we felt compelled to show our last respects to our dear *Mem*, if they would allow us into the house. We decided to wear our Amish clothes again to avoid drawing excessive criticism.

Pastor Stowe accompanied us to the visitation, which was a great comfort to us, and the younger aunts and

---

[21] I Corinthians 7:31, *And they that use this world, as not abusing it: for the fashion of this world passeth away.*

cousins were apparently glad to see our children. The evening went better than we had anticipated, but not without some confrontations by several relatives.

The next day the funeral was held in the big house on the home place. Of course, we were not allowed to sit with the relatives, as would have been normal in a funeral service. Several of John's former-Amish cousins and an Aunt attended as well. We enjoyed a wonderful time of fellowship with them after the service. Our entire shunned group was seated at a separate table at lunchtime. Our Lord was merciful in our time of sorrow, and though the atmosphere was dreadfully tense, the day went by relatively peaceful.

However, it was a grievance to us that some of the family would stoop to the level of accusing us of killing *Grosmommy* by breaking her heart. They were evidently ignoring the fact that her heart condition almost claimed her life on several occasions years earlier.

In August, we packed the old station wagon with some camping gear, took our two children, and headed out on a two-week vacation to the beautiful Colorado mountains. We were immensely enjoying our liberty in Christ. With a great sense of freedom in the Lord, we were able to go wherever we desired, without hiring a driver. There was no *Ordnung* to prohibit us from enjoying God's magnificent creation.

We had a very enjoyable time indeed, in spite of traveling the wrong way on a one-way street and frantically trying to find our way out of Denver. We did not wish to ever repeat that part of the adventure in the future. It was truly a hands-on training in the realm of traveling. God patiently protected us greenhorns countless times, as we went zigzagging across this great land of freedom.

We were barely aware that we were roughing it by sleeping in the back of our vehicle at a KOA campground. Eventually, we bought a tent for future vacations. That was only the first of numerous vacations we took to the majestic mountains of Colorado.

John was still working various odd jobs wherever he could find work until fall, when he started working at a local sawmill. The pay increase was a blessing, although still rather minimal.

Our first experience in purchasing a home took place that fall after having lived with Glen and Ida for eight months. They had graciously turned a couple of their upstairs bedrooms into living quarters for us a few weeks after we moved from Bowling Green. May our Lord forever bless them for their great sacrifice! That left more room for Ervin's family in the rental house.

The house we bought was rather dilapidated and in great need of repair, and in our new culture, with our meager income at the beginning, we could not afford to do remodeling immediately. Learning to make the best of the situation was not new to me, having grown up without much. Nevertheless, we now had the Lord, and He met our every genuine need. By and by He increased our financial blessings over the years.

Our three oldest children have many fond memories of living on that first thirty-acre farm. Since it was beside the South Fabius River, they spent many hours playing in its shallow waters. Its clear, cool, refreshing stream was a pleasant relief to them on sultry summer days.

However, that same calm source of enjoyment could also transform into a roaring torrent, resembling the mighty Mississippi. At numerous times, our access to the road was closed due to its raging waters, which knew no boundaries. If flooding was predicted, we usually had to park our vehicle beside the road, up on the hill, in advance. We would then walk out through the field on higher ground to the vehicle when we needed to use it.

In December, we celebrated the birth of Christ. That included the experience of finding our first Christmas tree. What great fun the children had, helping their *dat* search all through the woods for that perfect tree. At last, they settled on a little three-foot evergreen, which we carefully placed on top of our treadle sewing machine in the living room window. After adding a few trimmings, we each had a gift or two to place under it, reminding us of the gift of Christ to us.

In February of the next year, we were blessed with another baby girl, Loretta Sue. Since our house was old and difficult to heat, we kept the baby's bassinet in the living room close to the wood stove.

A new baby was an interesting experience in our new culture. Many of the church people gave baby clothes and other baby items to help us get started, which was a great blessing. At two weeks old, we dedicated her to our Lord during a church service. Our prayer was that He would bless her, and the rest of our children, as they grew up to serve Him.

John's *dat* passed away in March of 1987, three years after we moved to Maywood. At the age of seventy-three, his strong medium-build frame was no match for the dreadful leukemia that claimed his life after only a short illness. He had been remarried for only four and a half months.

When we went to his funeral, we were received in much the same manner as we were at John's *mem's* funeral almost three years earlier, with some admonishing from relatives and acquaintances.

That fall, a household auction was held for *Dat's* Amish children only. That auction was followed by a two-day public estate auction. Scores of items were sold that he had accumulated over forty years of going to various public farm auctions himself.

He had filled a couple of machine sheds with his bargain farm machinery for his seven sons to buy, or simply for spare parts to repair those already in use. He was a very generous man and found great joy in giving things to his children, as well as to other people in the community.

We attended one of the public auctions, but it was rather sad to see the farm machinery, livestock, and so many of the old familiar pieces of furniture, books, dishes and more being sold, while we were not allowed to bid on anything. We were not permitted to buy even a small item, since they were not allowed to receive money from us. That was part of the shunning practices enforced by the church.

The proceeds of all the auctions and the large real estate were divided among their twelve Amish children only. The other three, Joe (and Rachel), John (us), and Elizabeth (and Ervin) were not included in the will to receive any inheritance from the estate. However, we could rejoice in a much greater inheritance, which would last for all eternity. *Knowing that of the Lord ye shall receive the reward of the inheritance: for ye serve the Lord Christ* (Col. 3:24). *Giving thanks unto the Father, which hath made us meet to be partakers of the inheritance of the saints in light* (Col. 1:12).

No one, not even a religion, could take that inheritance from us. It will not rust, deteriorate, be stolen, be awarded unfairly, decrease in value, cause family feuds, nor can the government seize it. The Scripture clearly reminds us that it *fadeth not away,* and is *reserved in heaven for His children.*[22]

God sometimes allows events to occur in the course of our lives that we cannot understand, but He is always working for our good. He tells us in Jer. 29:11, *For I know the thoughts that I think toward you, saith the Lord, thoughts of peace, and not of evil, to give you an expected end.* Even when it seems much is lost from an earthly perspective, God can work mightily through our circumstances, allowing us to inherit rich eternal blessings, and bring glory to Him.

We encouraged each other with those wonderful Truths, and determined to trust our Lord to meet our every earthly need. He has never, nor will He ever, fail us. Matthew 6:33 says, *But seek ye first the kingdom of God, and his righteousness; and all these things shall be added unto you.*

Likewise, Psalms 23:1 says, *The LORD is my shepherd; I shall not want.* We shall have no lack since He is our Shepherd.

God has blessed us immeasurably in the spiritual, physical, and financial aspects of life since we were adopted into His family twenty-five years ago. Through His Word He gave us the blessed assurance of being His children even now. Romans 8:16 says, *The Spirit itself beareth witness with our spirit, that we are the children of God.* We notice it says *we are,* which is in the present tense, rather than will be. Also, I John 5:12 gives us that assurance: *He that hath the Son hath life; and He that hath not the Son of God hath not life.* We take *hath* to mean now, not only in the future.

---

[22] I Peter 1:3-4, *Blessed be the God and Father of our Lord Jesus Christ, which according to his abundant mercy hath begotten us again unto a lively hope by the resurrection of Jesus Christ from the dead, to an inheritance incorruptible, and undefiled, and that fadeth not away, reserved in heaven for you.*

Another great blessing and joy over the years has been the privilege of witnessing the results of our relentless prayers. With exceeding gratitude, we now experience more peaceful visits with my family in their Amish home in Michigan. Our Lord and Savior is all powerful, and nothing is too hard for him.[23]

Our Lord has also blessed us with three adult children who, by His grace, are dedicated servants for Him in various areas of life.

In more recent years, he gave us two more sons, who are still at home, in the "training field," and we eagerly wait to see what God's plan is for their lives. We have dedicated them to our Lord, and we pray He will use them to His glory, in the way that He chooses.

At a young age, each of our five children accepted Christ as their Lord and Savior.

God has given each of our three adult children a wonderful born-again partner in marriage. Rosa is married to Tom, and God has called them to live close by and serve Him by raising a godly family. Omar married Tracy, and they have been called to serve our Lord as missionaries, taking the Gospel to Brazil. Loretta and her husband Paul J. have been called of our Lord to spread the Gospel in Baffin Island.

Had we not made that life-changing decision at the crossroads we encountered twenty-five years ago, our children would not have been available to hear our Lord's call. God in His omniscience had a plan and brought each

---

[23] Jeremiah 32:17, *Ah Lord GOD! behold, thou hast made the heaven and the earth by thy great power and stretched out arm, and there is nothing too hard for thee.*

of us to where we are today serving Him in various Gospel-preaching, soul-winning, conservative Baptist churches.

We do not understand why God loved us so much that He gave His Son for us. Galatians 2:20 is one of my favorite verses in all the Scriptures: *I am crucified with Christ: nevertheless I live; yet not I, but Christ liveth in me: and the life which I now live in the flesh I live by the faith of the Son of God, who loved me, and gave himself for me.*

He has freed us from the yoke of bondage, and Galatians 5:1 reminds us to stand fast in that liberty: *Stand fast therefore in the liberty wherewith Christ hath made us free, and be not entangled again with the yoke of bondage.* John 8:36 tells us, *If the Son therefore shall make you free, ye shall be free indeed.* We are no longer the servants of law and sin, but of our Savior Jesus Christ.

We cannot comprehend why the Creator of this universe, the sovereign, holy, and altogether righteous Judge of all mankind desires our fellowship. Only our great Redeemer can possess a love so deep that *He brought me up also out of an horrible pit, out of the miry clay, and set my feet upon a rock, and established my goings. And he hath put a new song in my mouth, even praise unto our God: many shall see it, and fear, and shall trust in the LORD. Blessed is that man that maketh the LORD his trust...* (Psalms 40:2-4).

Many, O LORD my God, are thy wonderful works which thou hast done... (Psalms.40:5).

What shall I render unto the LORD for all his benefits toward me? (Psalm 116:12).

Our Lord's merciful goodness and everlasting love inspires us to endeavor to keep Him supreme in our lives. We realize Satan works diligently to gain that position. The Lord also deserves the best of our time, rather than our spare time.

May all who read our testimony get a true glimpse of our almighty loving Lord and Savior, and His mercy and grace in our lives and in the lives of others who have entrusted their souls to Him. We are truly unworthy of Him.

The sincere desire of our hearts is that some lost soul might see his or her need to bow the knee before the King of Kings and Lord of Lords and accept Him as Savior. He wants to be your Heavenly Father, so that you may *worship Him in spirit and in truth.* John 4:24 tells us, *God is a Spirit: and they that worship Him must worship Him in spirit and in truth.*

In II Peter 3:9, we see our Lord's will for every soul: he is *not willing that any should perish, but that all should come to repentance.*

How it must grieve our Lord to cast into an eternal hell those for whom He shed His blood and died. But they rejected Him, attempting to join their own righteousness with His. Romans 10:3 says, *For they being ignorant of God's righteousness, and going about to establish their own righteousness, have not submitted themselves unto the righteousness of God.*

No one is so sinful that the Lord will not save them. *For God so loved the world, that he gave his only begotten Son, that whosoever believeth in him should not perish, but have everlasting life* (John 3:16). Nor is anyone so good that the Lord need not save them. For *all have sinned, and come short of the glory of God* (Romans 3:23).

What our Lord has done for our family, He will do for anyone who will simply accept Him as Lord and Savior of their life. It is a personal choice that one must make to inherit eternal life.

It is no secret what God can do.
What He's done for others, He'll do for you.
With arms wide open, He'll pardon you.
It is no secret what God can do.

Song by Stuart Hamlin

Did You Know...

✓ In some communities long vacation or sightseeing trips are frowned upon as a worldly pleasure and unwise use of money.

✓ Today some less conservative Amish churches permit the use of a community freezer, powered by a generator, along with gas stoves and refrigerators in the kitchen.

✓ The Amish believe in lifestyle evangelism and do not send out missionaries to take the Bible to foreign countries or start churches there.

✓ Most Amish people believe they cannot know their eternal destiny until they have died and stand before God. It is only then that they expect to find out whether their righteous deeds will balance God's scales of righteousness. Their hope is that God will balance it with His grace where they are found lacking.

Our family in 1984

Funeral procession

View from our former front yard to the barns

Sale day crowd between our former house and big house

All our children, in-laws, and grandchildren, 2009

Enjoying our five precious grandchildren

In Summary

When my husband and I say that we are born again, we are not boasting of ourselves or of anything we have done. It is entirely the result of what Jesus has done for us.

Following is a brief review, explaining what we believe the Bible teaches us about man's relationship with God.

God's Purpose for Us:

The Bible says God created man to worship, serve, and fellowship with Him—a perfect relationship. Rev. 4:11 says, *Thou art worthy, O Lord, to receive glory and honor and power: for Thou hast created all things, and for Thy pleasure they are and were created.*

Mankind's Sin Problem:

Adam chose to sin against God rather than serve Him in the garden of Eden, destroying that perfect relationship between God and man. Consequently, the whole human race is born in sin. *Wherefore, as by one man sin entered into the world, and death by sin; and so death passed upon all men, for that all have sinned* (Rom. 5:12).

As it is written, there is none righteous, no, not one (Rom. 3:10). *For all have sinned, and come short of the glory of God* (Rom. 3:23).

Penalty of Sin:

The Bible also says there is a penalty for sin. It is spiritual death, or eternal separation from God. *For the wages of sin is death; but the gift of God is eternal life through Jesus Christ our Lord* (Rom. 6:23). The soul separated from God is lost and destined for hell as we see in Rev. 20:15: *And whosoever was not found written in the book of life was cast into the lake of fire.*

Christ's Payment for Sin:
The Bible says that Jesus Christ, God's sinless Son, came to pay the penalty for our sins when He died on the cross in our place, was buried, and rose again the third day.
But God commendeth His love toward us, in that, while we were yet sinners, Christ died for us (Rom. 5:8).
And that he was buried, and that he rose again the third day according to the scriptures (1Cor.15: 4).

Free Gift:
Throughout all times humans have tried many different ways to gain or earn eternal life, but all attempts have been and always will be unsuccessful. Scripture tells us, *Not by works of righteousness which we have done, but according to His mercy He saved us…* (Titus 3:5). It is *not* even partially by man's effort.
For by grace are ye saved through faith; and that not of yourselves: it is the gift of God: not of works, lest any man should boast (Eph. 2:8-9).

God's Promise of Eternal Life:
We also learned that God promises salvation to all those who receive Him. Jesus Christ Himself said, *Verily, verily, I say unto you, He that heareth my word, and believeth on him that sent*

me, hath everlasting life, and shall not come into condemnation; but is passed from death unto life (John 5:24).

…Believe on the Lord Jesus Christ, and thou shalt be saved… (Acts 16:31).

For whosoever shall call upon the name of the Lord shall be saved (Rom.10: 13).

Repentance and Receiving the Savior:

We learned that Christ's payment for sin would not count for us until we personally received Him as our own Lord and Savior.

To receive Him, we realized we had to acknowledge our lost condition, repent of sin and trusting all else. *Repent ye therefore, and be converted, that your sins may be blotted out…*(Acts 3:19). *I am the way, the truth, and the life, no man cometh unto the Father, but by me (John 14:6). But as many as received him, to them gave he power to become the sons of God, even to them that believe on his name* (John 1:12).

We then bowed our knees, confessed our sinfulness to Jesus Christ, asking Him to cleanse our sinful hearts and be our Lord and Savior. Our black sinful hearts were made white as snow through the blood of Christ. We are no longer lost sinners, but saved sinners.

Now as His child, we can have our daily sins forgiven and have blessed fellowship with our Lord. *If we confess our sins, he is faithful and just to forgive us our sins, and to cleanse us from all unrighteousness* (I John 1:9).

Only as His child do we have the Holy Spirit's power to serve and please Him. *So then they that are in the flesh cannot please God* (Rom. 8:8). *But without faith it is impossible to please Him* (Heb. 11:6).

In Summary   149

The Greater Inheritance

For information, questions or comments write to:

Calvary Books
31056 State Hwy. C
La Grange, MO 63448

To order additional copies go to:
www.thegreaterinheritance.com

Or send check or money order to
above address, please.